D0682398

Managing
Home
Alteration
and
Extension
Projects

Managing
Home
Alteration
and
Extension
Projects

Julian Owen

The Crowood Press

First published in 2012 by
The Crowood Press Ltd
Ramsbury, Marlborough
Wiltshire SN8 2HR

www.crowood.com

British Library Cataloguing-in-Publication Data
A catalogue record for this book is available from the British Library.

ISBN 978 1 84797 316 0

Typeset by Jean Cussons Typesetting, Diss, Norfolk
Printed and bound in Malaysia by Times Offset (M) Sdn Bhd

Contents

Dedication

This book is dedicated to Nic Antony, John Ball, Steve Buttler, Mukesh Hotwani, Duncan Mathewson, Denise Mathewson, Philip McCulloch, Jason See and David Thorp, all of whom are directors of the ASBA Architects' network and have given much time and energy over the past eighteen years to ensure its success.

Acknowledgements

I would like to thank the following for their assistance in preparing this book:

Richard Owen for his helpful comments and editorial eye.

The staff of Julian Owen Associates Architects who have worked on most of the projects featured in the book.

The members of the ASBA Architects' network who have provided constant advice and support.

Unless otherwise credited, all illustrations and projects are by Julian Owen Associates Architects.

CHAPTER I

What Are Your Options?

What To Do at This Stage

1. Decide whether you wish to stay in the house or move.
2. Look at how much you can afford to spend.
3. Consider the options, e.g. extension, loft conversion, etc.
4. Work out approximate cost of the work.
5. Get financial advice.
6. Work out a provisional timetable.
7. Talk to professionals, e.g. architect.

Your home is probably the biggest investment that you will ever make. Apart from the cost there is usually an emotional investment as well because our hopes, dreams and even sense of self-worth are often woven into its fabric. After moving two or three times, most families prefer to stay put, so altering and improving houses is a favourite pastime in the UK. If you consider all the problems that arise when you move, involving school catchment areas, payment of stamp duty, moving costs, dealing with estate agents and getting to know new neighbours, it easy to understand why many of us prefer to make the best of what we have. On top of

Typical house before extending.

all this, we are bombarded by TV programmes and magazine articles telling spellbinding stories of how dull houses can be transformed into beautiful homes by intrepid DIY enthusiasts, apparently at almost no cost. The darker side of the media coverage relates the equivalent of the fireside horror story for the modern consumer, with endless tales of wicked builders ruining the lives of their innocent victims.

If you are thinking of taking the plunge and starting your own home-improvement project, but want the real story of how to be successful, this book is for you. It distils all the practical information needed to get a project up and running, with some warnings about the pitfalls along the way. It will also provide you with some creative inspiration.

TOP: **Typical house after extending.**

MIDDLE: **House before extension.**

BOTTOM: **House after extension.**

FEASIBILITY STUDY – SHOULD YOU MOVE HOUSE INSTEAD?

Somehow, you have to get your project started and move from general discussions to making a realistic assessment of your best options. In short, you need to carry out a 'feasibility study'. This involves looking at why, when and how the improvements could be made. If done methodically, it will also help you to decide if they are worth doing at all. Too many families embark on a lengthy house-alteration project, only to find, at the end of a stressful and costly few months, that it has not worked out as well as they hoped. Such failures are usually due to a lack of proper consideration of the options right at the very start, before work on the project starts in earnest. The end result of a feasibility study may be that you should not proceed, because it would not be right for the building or would be too expensive. So it is vital to confront all the important questions early.

Instead of assuming that the answer to your problems is to get the builders in, the simplest solution – to just move house – should be properly considered. Why are you thinking of making the changes? What are the costs and the benefits that are likely to result? If your motive is to make a nice profit, think again. Most home-renovation projects do not add more than their cost to the value of the building. It may actually be less risky to put the money towards a new house on the next step up the ladder. There are ways of making a profit, of course, but these depend on the design, location and condition of the house. If you have good DIY skills, you can save money by doing a lot of the work and management of the project yourself, provided that you have the free time. You can also get the best value for your money by thinking of ways to improve the desirability (and therefore sale price) of the building.

If you decide to go ahead, start by considering the improvement in your lifestyle you are looking for rather than the exact type of alteration. For

The work involved in a loft conversion is often underestimated, but it can still be cheaper than moving.

Does It All Add Up?

This example shows how to calculate the cost-effectiveness of the work. At average 2011 prices, a typical loft conversion could cost £25,000 to £40,000 plus VAT. The new room-in-the-roof may only add £15,000 to £20,000 on to the value of a £180,000 house, which would mean a potential loss of between £5,000 and £25,000 if the house is to be sold straight after the work is finished. It is a similar story for many conservatories and extensions that usually result in a loss or just break even. If you plan to move in a few years' time, estimate the cost of the work and compare it with the price that the house will sell for afterwards. You can then decide whether the financial implications justify the project. This may not be a big concern if you intend to live in the house for many years, but may persuade you hold off and put the money saved towards your next home. For example, if you lose £10,000 on paper, but live in the house for ten years, then it has cost you £1,000 per year. Since moving costs can easily be more than £10,000 this would be good value.

example, 'more space for the kids to play and peace and quiet for the parents' might best be solved by larger individual bedrooms, or a family room, or a playroom in an outbuilding separated from the main house. The right answer will depend on your family, how much you can afford and the limitations of the house itself, so all options should be at least considered, however briefly, before fixing on one solution.

MAKING A PROFIT

One factor that may affect your decision to pick a particular type of alteration for your home is the potential for generating a profit, or at least getting the best value out of the money that you have available. It is fine if you choose to improve the home in the way that suits you best, regardless of the cost-effectiveness, provided that you are fully aware of the financial implications. For example, many people intend to live in the house for as long as their health and circumstances will allow it. In these cases, making a profit on any work carried out is possibly only relevant to their offspring who may inherit their estate in due course. Alternatively, a young couple who are trying to work their way up the housing ladder, and intend to move in shortly after the work is complete, need to pay serious attention to the likely effect on the sale price of any work that they carry out, and compare it with the money (and time) it will cost them. This couple will also have to choose the house they buy very carefully, and have a clear idea of what sort of property has the potential to have value added in this way.

Making significant profit from improving a house is not easy, because there are plenty of other people looking for the same opportunities. Apart from the professionals, it has become a hobby for many people with spare cash, who no longer trust stocks and shares or pension funds. If you have the vision to come up with creative ideas that no one else has considered, and follow the discipline of the market, you will have an easier time and make more profit than your less imaginative competitors.

So which alterations have the best chance of making an increase in the value of the house more than the cost of carrying out the work?

Loft Conversions

Many people assume that converting a loft is a very cheap way to acquire extra space, but this is not necessarily the case. The work required to transform a dusty attic into a comfortable bedroom is more extensive than appears at first sight. The roof line may need altering, to allow space for a proper staircase. A dormer may be needed to provide adequate headroom. A thick layer of insulation has to be installed under the rafters, and flimsy joists designed to hold up a ceiling will have to be replaced with deeper ones strong enough to carry the extra floor loads. Space will have to be taken from the floor below to form the new staircase. The end result can be only a small net gain in space for some types of roof. In some situations it might be necessary to make substantial alterations to the roof structure.

Extensions

It is rare to make money by extending a house. Typically, about half to three-quarters of the investment is recovered when it is sold. If the existing property is substantially smaller than the surrounding homes, it may be justified as an investment. Also, an extension can be cost-effective if it solves a specific problem and improves the way that the house can be used, for example, by linking up an outbuilding to the main house or providing a first-floor bathroom. The addition of a garage can also pay for itself in areas exposed to bad weather, or in a city where security is an issue.

Extensions are most cost-effective if they increase the size of a house to blend into a street where houses are all much larger than the original.

Conservatories

In a similar way to an extension, the addition of a conservatory is probably not going to cover its cost. In most parts of the country, you will be lucky to get half its build cost back, unless you live in the South West, which bucks the trend. In this area, the better weather seems the most likely explanation for the potential profit of up to 30 per cent that can apparently be made. The most cost-effective way to build a conservatory is to buy a kit from a builder's merchant and either pay a builder or build it yourself, as opposed to using a conservatory supplier.

Replan

Sometimes it is possible to improve the space planning of a house, or even increase the number of bedrooms, without having to build on to it. Agents tend to value properties according to how many bedrooms they have, rather than the floor area alone, so if a disproportionately large bedroom can be split into two moderately sized rooms for a relatively small outlay, the value of the house can be enhanced significantly. A classic example of improving a first-floor plan is where an old house has had a bathroom extension, which is only accessible through a bedroom. Using a partition to form a separate access to the bathroom from the landing results in a more saleable house.

Refit the Bathroom

If the existing bathroom fittings are in reasonable condition and you want to use your money effectively, it is not worth replacing them unless they are unattractive. If a new bathroom is necessary, the fittings should be white if you want them to appeal to the widest number of potential purchasers. For larger properties, adding a new en suite bathroom may be appropriate. According to a study by Cheltenham and Gloucester building society, new bathrooms are particularly prized in the North of England, where there is the potential to add 20 per cent over the installation cost to the house value of the house.

TOP: **Kitchen before refitting.**

BELOW: **Kitchen after replanning and refit.**

New Kitchen

Estate agents will tell you that attractive kitchens are a major selling point for any house and, if chosen carefully, a new one can justify its cost. As ever, the design must be pitched to match the size and quality of its situation. First impressions are important, so it is worth employing a joiner who is capable of achieving the standard of workmanship required, which is high. Poorly joined work surfaces and doors that are wonky will be exposed by the high lighting levels usually found in a kitchen. However, the same end result can sometimes be achieved by a thorough clean up and fixing some new doors on to the old units.

Decoration

For a neglected property, the most cost-effective work is a clean up and decoration inside and outside. A few hundred pounds spent in this way can add up to 5 per cent to the sale price. The impulse to let your creative instincts go wild must be firmly resisted here, because you should effectively create a blank canvas on to which prospective owners can imagine their own ideas. This means neutral colours everywhere; although white is too clinical and should be confined to the ceiling. Light colours make a room seem bigger, as do strategically placed large mirrors.

Garden

There are few things that can be done with the average garden to add significant value to a house, other than keeping it tidy. The main exception is the addition of a new drive. In areas where on-street parking is restricted or available spaces are oversubscribed, adding a car space can give a return of two and a half times the cost.

Maintenance

Boring though it may seem, basic maintenance and repairs of the property are essential, particularly where the defects are visible. You may get a few of them past potential purchasers by some cunning concealment, but they will be picked up the surveyor later on and used to negotiate a reduction in the sale price.

Double-Glazing

This will not normally pay for itself, unless the existing windows are rotten, past their useful life, or of the old-fashioned steel-framed variety. Installing UPVC replacement windows in a period house could appear to be out of character and may even reduce the value of the property. Creating a completely new window to light up a dark area, such as a stairwell, can be worthwhile.

Home Improvements

Most Cost-effective

- Maintenance and redecoration, when the house is currently in poor condition.
- Splitting a very large room into two medium-sized ones.
- Combining two very small reception rooms into one.
- Improving access between rooms, e.g. accessing a main bathroom off the landing rather than through a bedroom.
- Replacing poor quality bathroom or kitchen fittings with modest new ones.
- A thorough clean of the house, inside and out.
- Redecoration, where the existing condition is poor.
- Adding central heating, if it's not there already.
- Adding a parking space in the garden, if there is no off-street parking.
- A new garage to replace driveway parking.

Less Likely to Cover Their Costs

- Adding an extension.
- Building a conservatory, especially if poorly sited.
- Replacing a bathroom or kitchen where the existing ones are in reasonable condition.
- New double-glazing where the existing single glazing is in reasonable condition.
- Adding a swimming pool.
- Stone cladding.
- Underfloor heating.
- New decking in the garden.
- Making the ground floor completely open-plan.
- Forming a new basement.
- Planting trees in the garden, or adding water features, or garden ornaments.

BUDGETING

Most people fund their project from a mix of savings and an addition to their mortgage.

Clearly, the first step in drawing up a budget is to find out how exactly much money you can call

on. Usually there is equity stored up in the existing house because the mortgage is less than the sale price of the building. Lenders may finance extensions and alterations in these cases, as long as the final value is not less than the total money owed (known as 'negative equity'). It is a mistake to take

How to Raise the Money

- Your own savings – but don't commit all your cash in case you need money at short notice in an emergency.
- Family friends and relatives. If they are wealthy enough, this may be a way of raising the money. They may take a personal interest and may even want a say in how the project is run.
- Credit card – to be avoided unless for a very short-term emergency, due to the high interest rate.
- Mortgage increase – the safest and usually most cost-effective method. There will be administration charges and you will have to justify the project to the lender.
- Bank loan – an ordinary loan is not ideal for a home-improvement project, but some do provide loans specifically for this kind of project.
- Builder's scheme – usually much higher interest rate and less favourable terms than high street lenders. To be avoided.
- Independent financial advisor or broker. A specialist, independent broker may be able to help, by negotiating a good deal on your behalf, particularly if you are self-employed. There will be a charge for their services.
- Grants – disabled. If the alterations improve conditions for a disabled person (building regulations fees may also be waived by the local authority).
- Grants – renovation. There are local authority and government schemes that finance energy efficiency measures.
- Grants – conservation/historic buildings. A listed building may qualify for funding from English Heritage, but more often from the local authority – usually very small amounts.

Some of the costs incurred by home-alteration projects (2011 prices)	
Item	**Predicted Cost**
Contingency	At least 15 per cent of your budget is recommended at early stages.
Fees for design to planning application stage	These will vary according to the size and complexity of the project.
Planning application fee to local authority	£150
Planning appeal costs	Hopefully will not be needed. No fee for making the appeal, but may involve planning consultant's fees for preparing your case.
Fees for design to building regulations stage	Will vary according to the project size and complexity.
Building regulations plans approval fee to local authority	Typically £150 to have the plans approved and £125–£490 for site inspections (depends on size).
Fees for design work to tender stage	Will vary according to the project size and complexity.
Structural engineer's design work	Typically £200–£400.
Expenses for design work, e.g. printing costs, etc.	Typically £20–£50.
Finance costs	For extension to a mortgage.
Furniture storage costs	May be needed if several rooms out of commission.
Insurance costs, e.g. contents during building work	Can be very low or nothing.
Party wall surveyor	If a neighbour is affected by the work and party wall legislation applies, a surveyor is usually needed to sort it out.
Building work cost	A guess until tenders are obtained.
New kitchen	Usually by specialist rather than the builder.
Architect's contract management fees	May not be needed for smaller projects.
Remedial work to neighbour's property affected by the works	The Party Wall Act may force you to do this, regardless of the cost.
Temporary accommodation	You will have to rent somewhere if the house is uninhabitable during major works.
Landscape, planting and surfacing	Can mount up quickly if hard paving such as brick pavers or retaining walls are needed.
New furniture	Most people buy this for the new spaces.
If kitchen is out of commission for a long period during work, costs of meal out, ready meals, fast food, launderette, etc.	May be the only way to compensate for the loss of this essential facility.
Total Cost	**e.g. £35,000**
Budget Minus Total Cost	**e.g. £38,000–£35,000 = £3,000 under budget**

on a mortgage that you will struggle to pay if the improvements add little value to your home. The worst case is that you will be forced to sell the house and be left with a debt after paying back the money owed to the lender.

Never take up loan offers from specialist home-improvement companies or builders without looking at all the other options and getting alternative advice first. These loans pay out large commissions, are usually on far less favourable terms than the high street lenders and should be avoided. Ironically, if you are in the fortunate position of funding the whole project from savings, then you are in more danger than most of going along the wrong track, since you won't have to make a case for what you want to do and persuade anyone to lend you the money. Find a professional who is prepared to give unbiased financial advice and will be honest with you, rather than try to talk you into unnecessary expenditure.

Once you know how much you can raise, deduct 10–15 per cent from it immediately, before you start to think of ways to spend it. This is your contingency to allow for your own mistakes in calculating a budget and as an insurance against the things that go wrong over the course of the project. Whenever a problem is uncovered, at the design or the construction stage, the easiest way to solve it is usually by spending more money. If your initial budget assumes that you will spend every penny you have available, this will cause financial problems later on if you have underestimated the cost, which may take the shine off your enjoyment of a newly-improved home. A good discipline is to prepare a budget sheet at the earliest stages, even if it includes some fairly tenuous guesses. It can be updated as you progress and gradually get a more certain indication of the real costs. This process should continue until the builders leave the site. An easy mistake is to forget to allow for items related to the project that cost money, but are not directly involved with the building work, such as local authority fees and finance costs.

Most of the money will go on the building work but this is the most difficult to calculate at the beginning. It is easier to estimate figures for new building work than it is for alterations. Sometimes unforeseen problems are encountered when the existing structure and construction is exposed. Experienced professionals use price/m^2 or price/ft^2 to calculate approximate costs for extensions. For example, if a typical middle-quality extension costs £120/ft^2–£150/ft^2 (£1,290/m^2 and £1,615/m^2 respectively) at 2011 prices, multiplying the area of the extension by this figure, then adding 'spot prices' for work to the existing house will give an estimate of likely costs. This method cannot be used for internal alterations to an existing building. This is why reputable professionals will be reluctant to give you a cost before you have drawings or a list of the work needed, because there is no way that even an approximate of cost can be calculated without them. Any builder who gives the impression that they can give an estimate confidently without such information is bluffing.

The less reliable the cost information, the greater the contingency that should be allowed. For this reason, you may have a contingency of 15 or even 20 per cent at the start of the project, but have reduced this down to 5 per cent by the time that building work starts.

Estimating Costs in the Early Stages of a Project

Managing the cost is the hardest part of any building project and going over budget is the single biggest risk that you face. At the early stages, the calculations will all be 'best guesses', but you should review the budget calculation at every key point in the process. As you progress, the figures will become more accurate as you add to your knowledge and start to get a clearer idea of actual costs. The current budget calculations should be at the forefront of your mind whenever you have a key decision to make. There is no doubt that many building projects run into difficulties late in the project, when the true costs are discovered.

Unfortunately, there is no magic formula that can guarantee you will not go over budget. But you can do a lot to reduce the risk of it happening. A popular but generally true mantra in the building industry is that a project can be any two out of cheap, fast and good quality, and the relationship between these three elements decides how much

Careful planning should prevent the budget being exceeded after work starts on site.

it eventually costs. Assuming that the project is not needed urgently, the real balance that has to be struck by most people is between cost and quality. No early cost-estimate can be relied upon for guidance unless you have a clear idea of the quality of the finished rooms that it allows for. There are several ways of getting early cost-estimates and the ideal is to use two or three of them and compare the results – which will almost certainly be contradictory.

If the figures suggested to you by builders seem very low, be suspicious, because there are no easy bargains in the construction business, and you really do get what you pay for. There are a few costs that you cannot influence like VAT and local authority fees, so you just have to accept them; but many are in your control, to a greater or lesser extent. The biggest single influence on the price of your home is you – how you run the project and the choices that you make as you do it. To set a budget, you need to pick a realistic target figure, and then aim for it. Then check it regularly as you work through the process and adjust your next actions accordingly.

Talk to Builders

Sadly, at the very beginning of a project, no-one, not even the smartest, most experienced local builder you can find, can tell you accurately what the cost will be at the same time as guaranteeing a level of quality. Such a person may be able to predict a range of cost with reasonable accuracy. However, if you were to engage them on the spot without a clear idea of a scheme and without agreeing a standard of materials and finishes beforehand, they would rely on adjusting the quality once the project is on site to ensure that the job will make a profit for them. This is why many prices stated by builders at this stage are fairly heavily qualified. As a result of the uncertainty, it is not unusual to get wildly differing prices at this early stage, which can add to the confusion rather than be helpful. The better organized firms may be able to provide a schedule of the standard fittings and finishes that they use for their projects and will help you judge cost versus quality. Advice on how to find reliable builders and get prices that can be properly compared is offered later in this book.

Ask an Architect

Like builders, architects who do this type of work will also have some knowledge regarding the likely cost of a conversion, but will have a similar problem trying to make an accurate prediction. If you employ an architect directly, they will obtain fixed prices from builders using very detailed information about the project, but this will not be until later in the process. Architects tend to work with a wide range of builders and may be able to advise which of them will suit your likely budget.

Pricing Books and Quantities

It is the job of quantity surveyors in the building industry to estimate cost. They are not magicians, producing figures from the ether, but methodical professionals who break down any building project into a list of work and then use their knowledge of current prices to calculate the overall costs. Information on building costs is collated nationally by organizations such as the Royal Institution of Chartered Surveyors (RICS) and can be obtained to a very high level of detail, with breakdowns given for every possible operation that may be needed on a building site. In the early stages of a project, quantity surveyors use average statistics, again compiled from real, recently completed projects across the country, to estimate typical costs per square metre. This information is available at great expense online, but also in book form. Most of the publications are too complex for smaller domestic-scale projects and relate to larger building sites, where costs are quite different to the average locally based builder working on private houses. However, there are a number of publications aimed specifically at the latter sort of work (see 'Recommended Reading'). So if you want to estimate the costs for yourself, and can buy or borrow one of these books, there are two approaches that you can use. The first is to look up the approximate costs per square metre for the closest project description to yours. For example, the following is a typical cost-estimate from a pricing book (based on cost information published in 2008):

Clear out existing loft including services, water tank, etc., insulate between rafters and to walls, plasterboard finish, softwood floor, new staircase, new electrics and heating, new dormer windows 4m × 5m in size: £1,000–£1,300 per m^2. To add two dormer windows allow £11,000.

Questions to Ask Regarding Prices Published in Books and Magazines

How current is the information? A book could take 6–12 months between writing and appearing on the shelf, so even if the publication date is recent, it could be out of date.

Do the prices relate to your area of the country? Prices vary significantly depending on where the project is, e.g. Wales may be generally 15–20 per cent cheaper than Greater London. Most of these books include ways of adjusting the typical prices to reflect the location of the work.

What is included in the price stated? Costs/m^2 include everything necessary to do the job, but are designed for typical situations and do not stand up to close scrutiny. For example, the difference between a conversion with six large roof windows and one with four smaller ones cannot be accounted for by a price for each square metre. Prices for individual operations should include materials and labour time, but what about disposal of debris and equipment? The builder's overheads and profit often have to be added on to the calculations before the total figure is reached.

What is the source of the information? The most authoritative cost information is compiled by surveyors' organizations, such as the BCIS, which is a cost information service run by the Royal Institution of Chartered Surveyors. They compile data sent in regularly by surveyors from across the country, as do some other organizations and publishers – but few of the suppliers of this cost data work for the very small builders who carry out loft conversions. Also, bear in mind that if you are going to use a small builder, they rarely use pricing books when preparing quotations, preferring to rely on their own experience, knowledge and judgement.

This is a useful ball-park figure to start off with, but be aware that there are shortcomings in this kind of estimate.

The second way of using the pricing books is to break the work down into as much detail as is possible at this stage, measure the extent of the work required and compile a detailed schedule listing every operation that will be needed and the area, volume or numbers involved for each of them. This is how builders should, in theory, work out their prices; it is fairly laborious and relies on estimates at the early stages, but can produce some useful information. If the project is to be a DIY exercise, these calculations will have to be carried out by the homeowner at some point anyway. It is only recommended for someone who is experienced in home alterations and who is used to lots of work with a pocket calculator or spreadsheet.

The biggest problem with pricing books is that most small builders do not use them to estimate their costs. They will use a mixture of experience, actual prices from subcontractors and guesswork.

Many popular magazines feature articles and tables suggesting building costs – these are generally unreliable and should never be used as the only basis for setting a budget for a real project.

Other People's Projects

Aside from being a good source of potential builders for your project, friends, relatives and acquaintances may be ready to show you around their new extension and share their costs of the venture with you. Assuming it is accurate, this is probably the best way to gauge the likely bill that you will face for you own project. However, be aware that, particularly if there was an over-spend, it is only human nature to talk up the project and omit some aspects of the cost rather than admit to having lost control of the budget.

FACTORS AFFECTING THE COST OF YOUR HOUSE

Project Size vs Quality of Specification

The bigger the area included in the project, the more it is likely to cost. The better the quality of materials and fitting, the more it is likely to cost. Both of these are in your control, and should be the subject of careful thought and examination. If you aim at the minimum quality to achieve the maximum size, you are likely to be disappointed because most people would not be happy with the very lowest standards of construction and finish. It is likely that you will want to increase the standards as building work progresses and consequently go over budget.

Cost-Effective vs Cheap

Be aware of the difference between these two concepts. For example, using what seems to be a very cheap material may lose you money in maintenance costs and in the long run turns out to be a very expensive choice. Buying the cheapest available will be a false economy if you end up with an unsatisfactory end-result, or could get a much better product for a small extra outlay, or you have to rip something out and replace it because it is so unattractive.

Finance Costs

How you arrange your finance, how good a deal you get and how interest rates fluctuate, will all affect your budget. Most people finance a home-alteration project by extending an existing mortgage. It may be a good time to shop around and move the mortgage for the whole house to a new lender with a better deal than the current one.

Don't Forget VAT!

It is a convention in the building industry not to include VAT in any prices quoted. It also helps some salesmen not to mention it particularly when discussing cost, although if it is to be charged, it should be stated clearly on any written quotation. Some smaller firms, especially those that leave a lot of the fitting out to their customers, may not be registered for VAT and will therefore not charge it at all. Also, if you own a listed building, any aspects of the work that are considered alterations (as opposed to maintenance) are zero-rated for VAT.

Management

How well you manage your project will be crucial to keeping on budget. Careful planning and taking care to research and consider decisions are all likely to improve your chances of keeping the costs down. The single simplest way to get good value is to ensure that when prices are quoted from competing contractors or suppliers, they are for exactly the same descriptions of work and materials, so that they can be accurately compared.

HOW TO KEEP ON BUDGET

With any one-off building project, there can be no certainty of price at the start. The people who do best financially are usually the ones who identify and manage the risks most effectively.

Be Realistic, Get Realistic Advice

The biggest problem you face in trying to control the budget is your natural optimism – few pessimists ever get to the point of actually embarking on this sort of project. Salespeople, pundits and professionals that suggest it will all be simple and profitable sound attractive and convincing. You may desperately want to believe that everything will be easy and you will end up with a wonderful addition to your home that will cost very little. In short, a part of you wants to be lied to. Get lots of advice, read up as much as possible and then try to be brutally honest with yourself. Don't work to the most favourable figures you can find, but pick realistic ones. With a bit of luck, you may do very well financially, but count this as a bonus, and keep your expectations realistic.

Monitor and Discuss

Constantly revisit your budget, and keep doing this until the work is finished. Discuss it regularly with your family, professional advisors and builder. Keep your spreadsheet up-to-date by replacing your assumptions with real figures as you go along.

Control Small Decisions

It is quite rare for a single, big decision to be made that unexpectedly drives up costs. If you decide that the bath taps must be gold-plated, or that you need an extra dormer window, you will probably guess that it will cost more money. The main reason that costs go up is because of a range of what seem to be minor decisions is made, each of which on their own have a negligible effect on the total cost. But collectively they result in tender prices coming in over budget, and then they all have to be taken out of the contract. So small, apparently insignificant decisions have a cumulative effect. Be aware of the likelihood of this pushing you over budget and try to prevent it happening.

Have a Contingency

It cannot be stressed enough how important it is to have some financial reserves, for unexpected costs. At the very start of a typical project this amount should be a minimum of 10 per cent of the total budget. As building work is about to start and costs are more certain, it should be at least 5 per cent, preferably 10 per cent. It will be spent at some point, even if it is on a nicer bed or some fitted wardrobes right at the end.

Professional Team

Pick your team with care. If you are sufficiently self-aware, identify your own weaknesses and make sure that you get help to cover them. A good builder or architect will easily pay for themselves in money saved, quality achieved and stress relieved. A builder who is honest, reliable and efficient, but apparently more expensive, will usually be cheaper by the end of the project than another who quotes a very low price initially and has none of these qualities. The delight in getting building work for an extra low price will fade after a month or two, but the distress and irritation caused by cheap and shoddy workmanship may have to be lived with for many years.

Good Design

Design is not just about how things look. A well-planned design will get the best end result for your money. Good design will also ensure that problems are anticipated and designed-out where possible, allowing you to save money, or spend it on other aspects of the building. An ingenious designer will

Good design of an extension will increase the value of the completed building.

work out how to use the limited space available to its best effect and without excessive cost.

Preparation, Preparation, Preparation

You cannot be too well-prepared for building work to start. The more that has been worked out, agreed and specified in advance, the fewer extras there will be once the builder starts work and the better chance a project has of keeping to its budget.

Manage the Invitation of Tenders Correctly

The rules for obtaining prices are covered later in this book. If this crucial stage is not managed properly, the budget can go awry as building work progresses. If you choose not to get accurate tendered prices for the build, you will probably have to pay extra for this luxury. If there is only one

builder or supplier that you want, at least give them the impression that you are getting other prices to keep their price competitive.

Changes of Mind

If you change something after you have agreed a price, it will be a bit more expensive than if you asked for it to be included in the tender. If you change your mind after something has been built, it will be a lot more expensive. If you are unsure, you can ask for two or more different options to be priced as part of a quotation. If the doubtful item is a fitting or component, you can exclude it from the contract and give yourself the option of getting it from somewhere else. If you are completely undecided, identify it in the tender information as an item that may be changed, and get the builder to check with you before it is ordered or built.

Accommodation Costs

If the work to the house is extensive, you may have to move out. If this is necessary, don't forget to include the cost of renting in your calculations, and allow for the project over-running when agreeing a lease. A short increase in the rental period negotiated at the last minute can be expensive.

Get the House Surveyed Thoroughly

Potential defects in the house should be checked at an early stage in the preparation of the schedule of work. If a thorough survey is not carried out, in the hope that if there are problems they can be dealt with as the work proceeds, this may lead to increases in cost at a late stage in the project.

Never Pay in Advance

It may not be possible for this rule to be strictly applied in reality, because there may be some specialist components that are manufactured particularly for your project that will require a deposit of some kind. Otherwise, pay promptly, pay in stages, if appropriate, but pay after the service or product has been provided. If you pay a builder large sums up front, they may lose the incentive to make the completion of your project a priority or, in the very worst case, disappear without completing the work to your satisfaction.

Keep Good Records

If there are disputes about money, such as whether some aspect of the work is an extra or whether it was instructed by you rather than improvised by the workman on site, a combination of clear tender documents and some well-kept contemporaneous notes of meetings and discussions will help you to win the argument and avoid extra payments. Ensure that any changes to the original tender agreed before and during the building contract are confirmed to all parties in writing.

TIMESCALE

Often major home improvements take longer than people realize at the start. The wheels of local authority bureaucracy move slowly. Good builders are busy and are not able to start as soon as you would like. Although the time taken to complete a project will partly depend on its size, there are some tasks that require the same time regardless of scale, such as the planning-approval process. It generally takes eight weeks, regardless of whether it is a whole house or kitchen extension being approved. It is better to work to a realistic programme and aim to reduce it, than be over-optimistic and end up disappointed or frustrated.

Typical project times for a two-storey extension	
Early Stages:	
Feasibility study	4 to 6 weeks
Interview architects	
Building Survey, Sketch Design Submission of Planning:	
Application drawings	4 to 6 weeks
Planning process	8 to 12 weeks
Preparation of Working Drawings	4 to 6 weeks
Tender Process/Building Regulations:	
Approval (can be run in parallel)	4 to 6 weeks
Waiting for contractor to become available	4 to 6 weeks
Building Process:	
Construction period	15 to 18 weeks
Total time from inception to completion	46 to 64 weeks

Key People

You will have to deal with a range of individuals, officials and professionals to get your project designed and built. Here are just a few of them.

- **Estate Agent.** Can estimate the market value of the completed house before the building work is started.
- **Building Society Manager/Finance Advisor.** You will probably need finance, and you need someone familiar with the particular needs of your project.
- **Architect.** Can help with preparing a brief, designing the house, preparing local authority applications and choosing and managing the contractor on site.
- **Planning Officer.** The decision will be made by the senior planners or the planning committee of the local authority, but a planning officer can advise on what is likely to be approved and what may be refused.
- **Planning Consultant.** If you have a controversial application, or wish to appeal against a refusal, a planning consultant is trained in planning law, and employing one can improve your chances of success.
- **Structural Engineer.** Most projects involve structural alterations that need design work and calculations by an engineer.
- **Building Control Officer or Approved Inspector.** An application for approval under the Building Regulations is separate from the planning approval process. The Building Control Officer approves the application and inspects the work on site.
- **Landscape Designer/Contractor.** If your external works are extensive, you may need a specialist.
- **Party Wall Surveyor.** If an extension is built close to a neighbour's foundations, or affects the dividing wall, certain conditions apply and you are obliged by law to serve a Party Wall notice on them.
- **Contract Manager/Foreman.** This is the most important role of the whole project. With a small building company, this will be the person who runs the company.
- **Subcontractor/Tradesman.** Strictly speaking, a subcontractor is employed by a building contractor, but the term is often used to describe anyone with a specialized skill or trade.
- **Supplier/Manufacturer.** If you are personally specifying products, you will want to deal directly with the suppliers. Most are happy to provide literature, samples and advice.
- **Builders' Merchant.** These are good places to see samples of products and materials and gain valuable advice on using them.

GET SUPPORT FROM THE WHOLE FAMILY

Assuming that you have a family, everyone will be affected by the building work and it is a good idea to involve everyone when the early decisions are being made. The more committed people feel, the easier it will be to put up with the disruption and inconvenience caused by building work. But no project can be run well if every decision has to be debated until everyone is happy, so people have to be ready to compromise. One way to reduce family conflict is for different members to take on different roles, e.g. one looks after money matters and someone else takes on the role of choosing the furnishings. Kids can be encouraged to take part in the planning and decoration of their bedrooms.

CHAPTER 2

Making the Best of What You've Got

Once you have decided that you will be making some kind of alteration to your home, you need to take a critical look at the house and assess its potential. This could be a good time to arrange an initial consultation with an architect. Architects carry out a lot of alterations to homes, even on a quite modest scale, and their fees are relatively cheap compared to other professionals, such as solicitors, estate agents and builders. They can give you an idea of what would be practical and cost-effective and offer an objective view of the alternatives.

OUT, UP OR DOWN?

Sometimes it is obvious that you need a particular type of alteration, such as an extension or loft conversion, but even a brief look at all the alternatives at this early planning stage can sometimes save time and money further down the line.

Replan the Existing Rooms

You may have your heart set on a radical or significant change to your house, but before you launch into it, take a step back and ask whether you can get what you need without major structural alterations or additions. Often the most obvious way to solve a design problem is just to add extra space (and therefore cost) to the floor plan. Sometimes what is really needed is the advice of a skilled designer to re-arrange the rooms and spaces within the existing walls of the property. Large rooms can be split into two, small rooms can be knocked into one, circulation can be reconfigured and the end result is a house that is transformed and works better for its occupants. Occasionally the poor layout of a home is dramatically improved by relocating or redesigning the staircase, hallway and landing.

Extend

As long as there is space around the property, an extension is a very effective, if costly, way of improving your home. At the same time, other rooms can be altered to improve the function and design of the whole building. Alternatively, an extension will avoid disruption to the rest of the house during building work, until a wall is broken through to join the new to the old.

Conservatories

This is a special type of extension. The huge number of conservatories built in the UK is due to the skill of high-pressure salesmen, rather than their value for money. The advantage of modest conservatories added on to the rear of a property is that

TOP: **This house was easily extended, with minimum disruption to the occupants, before and after.**

LEFT: **A badly built conservatory will devalue your home.**

A conservatory that has been well-designed and built, and carefully sited, can add value.

the room that they are added on to, will not lose too much daylight. Badly sited conservatories, of which there are many, will overheat in summer and cost a fortune to heat in winter. Never buy a conservatory from a door-to-door salesman without shopping around and also looking at other improvements that you could make for a similar cost.

Loft Conversions

It is a common misconception that loft conversions are always cheap to build. They can be very good value for money with some types of roof design, but it is wrong to assume that they will necessarily be as good value for money as the alternatives. Sometimes an entire bedroom is lost on the first floor to fit in a new staircase. However, if there is no room to extend the house to the side or back, it may be the best option to add room.

Basements

In the centre of towns, or the central areas of cities where space is at a premium, the value of the land a house sits on is higher than in typical suburban areas. This means that the fairly drastic solution to excavate and create new space under the house, is more cost-effective. Adding a basement is a job for specialist contractors who have experience of this kind of work and is undeniably expensive (e.g. from £100,000 upwards). But adding a complete new floor to a house, increasing the total size by a third, may well justify the investment in central London, for example.

Demolish and Rebuild

If a house has major structural defects, or is on a large site for its size, or is in an area with very high land values or any alterations needed to the existing building are extensive, then demolishing and rebuilding from scratch is worth considering. In the UK, VAT is incurred on most home alterations (the exception is altering a listed building) but building a completely new house is zero-rated. A 20 per cent saving on the cost of the building work can be enough to make a new house better value than extensive alterations.

Sometimes the best option is to demolish the existing house and rebuild a new one to your exact requirements.

APPRAISE YOUR EXISTING HOUSE

Before settling on the best way to improve your home, you need to assess the strengths and weaknesses of the existing building. If you are doing this to improve your lifestyle, concentrate on those points that are important to you, not to an estate agent. Start by looking at the site that the house stands on and how it is related to its surroundings.

Neighbouring Buildings

Your house may be smaller than its neighbours, so a larger extension will not look out of place in the street. There may be an architectural style that you wish to match. If there is no consistency to the style and appearance of the surrounding buildings, it should make it easier for you to get planning approval for a more contemporary design.

Security

Overlooking by neighbours or passing strangers may reduce privacy, but they can also reduce the chances of a burglary. Any side or rear boundaries that have a footpath or road alongside (as opposed to a neighbour's garden) are a security risk, because they offer the opportunity for a thief to climb in and out of your site more easily than trying to force a front door that is easily seen from the road.

Looking on to the Site

How visible from the street is the house? If the area has active neighbours who value the quality of their streets, or planning approval is required, you will have to satisfy other people that any alterations you make are appropriate. A front extension may be visible to everyone and needs to be designed more carefully than if it is out of sight at the rear.

The View from the Windows

A view out of the house may be an asset if it is a wonderful view, or a disadvantage if it overlooks the local abattoir. If an extension reduces the privacy of neighbours, for example by allowing you to overlook their garden it will be harder to get planning approval.

Window sizes and locations should be carefully planned to frame and make the most of the views.

Roads and Footpaths

If there are roads or footpaths close to your house, where they will allow people to peer in through windows as they pass, the more private spaces such as bedrooms should be positioned on the other side of the house.

The Garden

A small garden may suffer if it is reduced further by a new extension. A side extension may block the way through to the back from the front garden. Sometimes badly designed new building work blocks out sunlight, or creates odd fragments of space that are cut off from the main garden.

Access and Vehicles

Where there is a limited number of on-street car parking spaces, creating a new access on to the front garden is a good investment and will add value to the property. In truth, most garages in the UK are used for household storage rather than cars.

Hard, surface materials, such as block paving, are expensive and tend to leave a garden looking bare and uninviting, if used to excess. A common alteration to a suburban home is to demolish an

Sunlight can be used to create a warm character for a room.

old garage in the rear garden and build a new two-storey side-extension, with a new master bedroom and a garage downstairs.

Use of Sunlight

Intelligent use of sunlight makes a big contribution to any house design. If you don't know it already, get a compass to orient yourself and observe over time to see which rooms get sunlight and when for different months of the year. If you don't want to wait that long, use a sun-finding compass, which predicts the direction and angle of the sun on any given day of the year. Which rooms and windows get sun at what time may influence the way that you arrange new rooms and spaces.

Services

Meters for services like gas, water and electricity, and manholes will all have to be accounted for and, if necessary, altered. Someone should establish the routes of underground services before work starts. Sometimes there are public sewers under private gardens that have legal restrictions on them to prevent you from building over or near to them. Usually the latter will have been picked up by a typical solicitor's search when the house was purchased, although the rules changed in October 2011, so you should still check yourself. There are also provisions in the Building Regulations, such as those that will allow you to build over some types of drain, but not to build over a certain type of manhole. If the drain is in the way and cannot be relocated, you may have to move the extension.

It is usually fairly straightforward to build over electric and gas supplies. The exception is when there is a main's supply to other houses running under your land. Internal meters are best relocated outside, if possible, and on the side of the house rather than the front; it may be possible to bury it in a box at ground level.

Ground Conditions

If the house is to have an extension, conservatory or basement added, this will involve some disturbance of the ground. The ground will have to support the new building work, so the ground conditions are an important element of the site that need to be investigated.

Subsoil Type

The subsoil is the zone immediately below the topsoil that supports the foundations. The type of subsoil will have a direct influence on the design and cost of the foundations. If there is any suggestion that the subsoil is poor, trial holes are an essential part of the investigation. Generally, a two-storey house will only need 600mm (2ft) wide concrete foundations if the ground is good, but it may be necessary to dig down to reach undisturbed conditions. The worst case is where the foundations

Filled ground, which is made up of backfilled rubble or previous construction work, cannot be used to support foundations.

need to be deeper than about 2.5 to 3m; in this instance, concrete mini piles may be more cost-effective.

Clay

To avoid damage to foundations in a clay area, they have to be at least 1m deep to drop below the shrinkage zone of the clay, rather than the minimum for good ground, which is about 600mm. Trees draw moisture from the ground, especially in summer; their roots penetrate deep into the ground and accentuate its seasonal wetting and drying. In turn, this magnifies the expansion and contraction of the ground. This effect continues for several seasons after the tree has been felled. So foundations in clay subsoil near trees need to be dug down below the influence of the roots in the ground. The very worst case would require a foundation down to 3.5m below the existing ground level, requiring mini piles rather than conventional strip or trench-fill foundations.

Filled Ground

To prevent the occurrence of damaging settlement, most foundations are built directly on to 'virgin' or undisturbed ground. Once the ground has been disturbed by excavations and backfilled, any foundations built on it will settle, causing the structure above to crack. In this situation, new foundations must be taken down below the area that has been excavated. Sometimes this has to be done with special foundations, adding many thousands of pounds to the cost of the project.

Contaminated Land

Contamination means that the land has within it chemicals or minerals that present a risk of harm to people or the environment. It is usually as a result of a previous use of the land, such as for a factory. If there is any suspicion that your house is built on such ground, expert advice should be sought before building.

A HOUSE HEALTH CHECKUP

Before design work starts, you need to identify those features of the house that you wish to improve and enhance, and to survey the building to identify any defects or shortcomings. There is little point in carrying out expensive alterations and adding new parts to the house if you fail to repair or replace any substandard areas of the building. Also, the type of construction of the different elements of the building may make your preferred type of alterations easier or more difficult.

If the new work is extensive and you employ an architect or builder, they should investigate the existing building construction and help you to decide what work will be needed. Otherwise, you may choose to employ a building surveyor and others to prepare formal reports for you. There are several types of survey that can be carried out, and some are more useful than others when contemplating a building project. The person preparing the report should be suitably qualified, and both of you should be quite clear what it will be used for. Most surveyors are a member of the Royal Institution of Chartered Surveyors (RICS) and will have these letters after their name if they are.

Valuation Survey

Otherwise known as a 'Homebuyer Report', this is a statement of the likely sale price of the house. These surveys are only suitable for a house that is already in reasonable condition. If the house has been poorly maintained, or there is anything to suggest that there may be hidden defects, a more thorough survey is essential.

Property Purchase Survey and Valuation

These go into a little bit more detail than a simple valuation, and should note any obvious defects that are visible from walking around the property. They are often heavily qualified by making recommendation for specialist surveys, such as for the electrical and plumbing system, concealed timber and asbestos.

Full Building Survey

A more thorough survey of the whole property, including a proper investigation of the condition of all the construction, is quite expensive and also disruptive, because the only way to inspect every-

For some buildings, a thorough survey is essential before starting work.

thing is to make holes in the walls, floor and ceiling. The extent of the work necessary is reflected in the high cost. If a building is in poor condition, or is very old, you might consider this sort of survey.

Structural Investigation

A qualified structural engineer is the best person to carry out this type of survey because it involves detailed investigation of the structure. Unless it is included in the brief, it does not include a survey of the condition of the general construction or the state of the fixtures, fittings and services. The term 'Structural Survey' is sometimes misleadingly used by surveyors and building societies to refer to a superficial survey of the building that does not include a full survey of the structure of the building.

Measured Survey

A measured survey accurately records the dimensions of the building and these are used to prepare scaled drawings. This is an important part of the design process and it is essential to get it done properly, because these drawings are the basis of everything that follows.

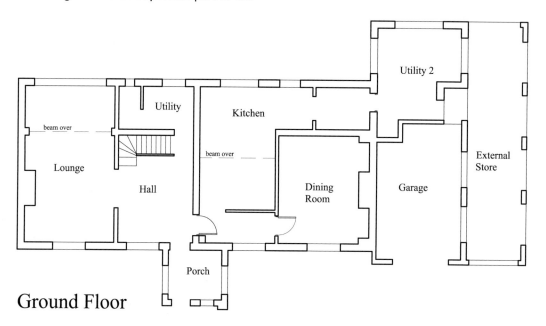

Ground Floor

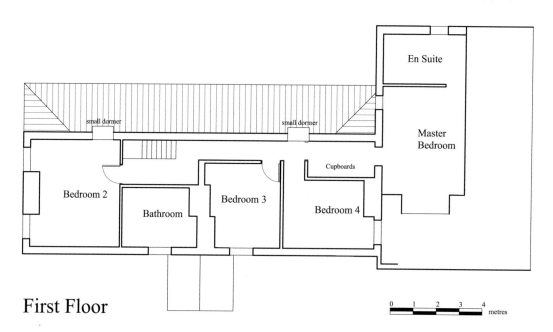

First Floor

An accurate measured survey at an early stage is essential.

Design

START WITH A GOOD BRIEF

Most people can guess that the success of a design partly depends on flair, ingenuity and practical thinking, but all good designers will add a further requirement to this list: a good brief. A design is unlikely to work well without time spent at the early stages making sure that everyone is clear what the finished project is expect to achieve. This may sound obvious, but too many design failures are caused by quick assumptions made right at the beginning of the process. If you are not clear on what your needs are, how can you expect anyone to design something that meets them?

The best briefs focus on what you need the new spaces to do for you, rather than necessarily listing the exact rooms and work that you think needs to be done. It is helpful if you can write down the aspects of the project that are important to you, and discuss them with your family in advance of a meeting with the architect.

An enjoyable and useful exercise is to compile a scrapbook of pictures of styles or designs that you particularly like. A similar collection showing things that you hate may avoid any misunderstandings with a designer. Decide your absolute minimum requirements, without which it is not worth your while to proceed. This is in contrast to those things that you would like, but would be prepared to sacrifice if practicality or lack of money makes them unattainable.

Record what extra space is needed and who will use it. Ideally you should try to indicate the sizes of any rooms that you think would meet your needs. You can estimate this by measuring the existing rooms in your house and visualizing how much has to be added. If you are not happy working out actual dimensions, you can relate back to existing rooms or features, for example, 'the Kitchen is to be 50 per cent larger, extended as far as the edge of the existing patio'.

Some Things to Include in Your Brief

Appearance

The style and appearance of your home are the most subjective things in the brief. The subject of style is highly emotive and may lead to the biggest disagreements between the family, but try to keep an open mind. One person's design feature is another's carbuncle. There is a huge range of choice of styles available, and some people find this intimidating. But everyone knows the styles and features that they don't like, so this is one possible starting point, and it is just as important to tell the designer these as it is to let them know what you do like.

A typical brief for an extension

Budget: £80,000–£90,000 plus VAT

Problems with existing house
Living room and kitchen are too small.
There is an unnecessary dining room.
An extra bedroom is needed.
The integral garage is used for storage and could be converted to a room.
The main bedroom needs an en suite bathroom.

Occupants
Husband and wife live in house, with one daughter.
Son comes to stay during university holidays.
Occasional visits from elderly relatives and family friends.
Several large dinner parties every year, including summer barbecue.

Essential extra space needed
New combined kitchen/dining/family space, larger than the combined existing spaces.
New bedroom upstairs, with the existing smallest bedroom becoming an en suite.

New rooms that would be desirable
Downstairs WC.
Detached garage to replace the one that has been converted.

Preferred location for extension
Side and rear.

Appearance
Contemporary feel to those parts not visible from the front.
Modern interior, open-plan downstairs.
High daylight levels, rooflights where possible.

Future
Allow for downstairs bedroom for dependent relative at a later date.

Work to existing house
New boiler.
Redecorate throughout.
Replace all existing windows with new UPVC.
Upgrade the energy efficiency of the house.

Other important considerations
House will be occupied during the building work.
Kitchen and bathrooms must be available all the time during the work.
We dislike: mock Tudor, glazing bars, patio decking and low ceilings.
The neighbours have expressed concern regarding our early ideas.
We are in a conservation area.

Attached: Extracts from several magazines showing design features that are particularly liked or disliked.

You need to decide early on in your project whether you want to contrast with, or match into, the existing style. Left, before; right, after.

Hot Tip

Keep a cheap camera in the car and quickly snap pictures if you pass anything that may be a useful clue to how you would like your conversion to look from the outside. But beware of angry house owners who may mistake you for a burglar 'casing the joint'!

The best way to record your inclinations is to find some illustrations – a picture really does say a thousand words. Cut out and keep photos from magazines. Keep a camera handy and take your own pictures of houses that interest you. If you have time, go around the show houses on the local new estates (with your camera). Talk to architects and designers, visit exhibitions and read as many magazines as you can get hold of.

Involve your family in the design of their rooms. Children particularly enjoy the chance to have an unusual space for their bedroom.

If you examine the information that you have collected, there are likely to be some consistent themes, e.g. particular styles and features that crop up more than others. Using these clues, you should be able to take a stab at listing your preferences.

Whose Room is It?

Who is likely to use a room is often obvious, but not always – asking this question may spark a discussion in the event of a disagreement. The family member who is going to use the room most should perhaps be allowed the final say on its design.

Furniture

At the beginning, you may not be sure what the fitted or loose furniture will go in the rooms, but it is worth making some educated guesses. Your designer needs to be aware of the likely contents of the room to plan it well and warn you if it will not fit. For example, with a loft conversion, you will have to be able to get beds and chairs up the stairs and then find space for them in rooms with limited headroom. A classic mistake in a loft is to allow space on the plan for a large double-bed, only to find once it is in place that there is not enough headroom to walk around the side to climb into it.

Electrics and Lighting

A regular complaint about many newly-created rooms is that they do not have enough electric sockets in the right locations. A little thought at an early stage regarding the technology that is likely to go in the room and the best positions for it, will help ensure that your conversion has enough power and phone sockets. Another area neglected in many homes is the ability of lighting design to contribute to the quality of rooms and spaces in the house.

Sustainability and Energy Efficiency

An issue that should be important to many is how 'green' or 'eco-friendly' the construction and design should be. If this is a high priority for you, it is vital to identify this as early as possible. Current building regulations already acknowledge the need to make modern homes respectful of the environment and natural resources. However, there are many ways in which you can improve on the minimum requirements – it is a question of how far you want to go, and how much you can afford. Sadly, many of the more radical options are expensive, and do not work out as economic for the average homebuilder, but by careful design it is possible to incorporate some of them at low cost.

You may need to do some investigation before you decide how far you want to go down the green route, and you may face some interesting dilemmas, usually as a result of the expense. If you have to choose between a luxury bathroom or a solar-power heating system, which would you go for?

ARCHITECTS AND DESIGNERS

All architects now use computers for the detailed design, because they are more efficient than using a drawing board.

It is worth spending a little time choosing the person or company who will play the crucial role preparing design and construction drawings. The architect must be able to understand your requirements, respect your budget and put forward ideas and suggestions in a clear way. As with any creative project, good communication between client and designer is vital. In turn, as the client you should make your requirements clear, as well as listen to your advisor's professional advice. But design skill and the ability to draw are not enough in themselves. You need someone who also understands how buildings are put together and has a profound knowledge of building construction. Many building projects look quite different in three dimensions, compared to their appearance on a two-dimensional drawing. Your architect must be able to visualize a design in three dimensions, and be capable of explaining this to you, in the form of sketches, perspectives and three-dimensional computer-aided animations, if necessary.

Hot Tip

Even modest, small-scale projects, such as a room refurbishment, can benefit from a trained designer's input. Most will agree that you can pay by the hour, so that you can use their design skills at the early stages for ideas and suggestions, without using them for the full service that is more appropriate to slightly bigger projects, such as an extension.

ARCHITECTS

Only designers who have completed a demanding seven-year course are allowed to use the title 'architect', because it is protected by law. People who use superficially grand titles, such as 'architectural consultants' and 'architectural designers', are unlikely to be architects and may have no formal qualifications or training at all. An architect's minimum seven-year training is the longest of any construction professional because, apart from design training, it includes all aspects of the construction process, including smaller to larger scale buildings. In addition, they are trained in construction contract law, project management, materials science and structural design.

Anyone who uses the title 'architect' must be registered with the Architects Registration Board (ARB), a government organization that ensures architects follow a code of practice and deals with complaints, as well as keeping a register of qualified architects. This provides valuable protection for consumers, but unfortunately the ARB has no power to discipline or fine non-architects if they are incompetent or dishonest. Most architects are

---

How to be a Model Client

1. Make sure that you and your family have a clear idea of the important elements of your brief before asking the architect to prepare a design.
2. Part of an architect's job is to think of things that may not have occurred to you, so don't dismiss ideas that conflict with your brief straight away, if there is a sound reason for proposing them.
3. You should put the fate of your house in the hands of someone with experience, expertise and skill, which are rare, so be prepared to pay a reasonable fee for the good service you will need.
4. Make yourself available during office hours for meetings with your architect and other consultants, if possible. To you it is a hobby, for them it is work.
5. If you are unhappy with something that your architect has done, raise it immediately and tactfully.

There are many different types of designer with varying levels of skill and qualifications who may be able to assist you with your project. Many types of people present themselves as being able to design houses, with varying levels of skill. There are many factors, apart from paper qualifications, that will decide who is right for your project.

Look for the logo. RIBA membership is a badge of quality. RIBA.

also members of the Royal Institute of British Architects (RIBA). Members of the RIBA are allowed to call themselves 'chartered' architects, because this organization has a Royal Charter. RIBA membership is held by individual architects. Some practices meet the higher standards of probity and practice management that allows them to be 'chartered practices'.

Architects don't just produce designs and pretty drawings. The reason it takes so long to qualify is that they also have extensive training and experience of practical construction methods, project management and contract law. Although their 'unique selling point' is design skills, architects actually spend most of their time designing construction details, sending out tender packages, running projects on site and dealing with contractors on their client's behalf.

Architectural Technologists

This title is not protected by law in the same way as architects but these professionals are usually members of the Chartered Institute of Architectural Technologists (CIAT), which requires its members to be fully trained and qualified in building construction. Academic training is not as lengthy, is less broad than for architects and concentrates mostly on the practical building-construction side. It is not essential to be a good designer to qualify, although some technologists acquire these skills through experience.

Surveyors

Surveyors may sell houses, estimate quantities, manage the construction of buildings or manage property. Although the formal training does not include much on aesthetic design, a few design houses. The title 'surveyor' is not protected and can be used by anyone, but trained, qualified surveyors are members of the Royal Institution of Chartered Surveyors (RICS).

Contractors

Some builders offer design services, but usually by using freelance designers. If you pay a builder to do the design, it usually means that you will be tied into using them to do the building work. You will not get independent advice this way, because the designer is there to help the contractor make a good profit, rather than protect your interests, and you can't get alternative quotes if you want to use the design.

Structural Engineers

Most projects of any significance need a qualified engineer to carry out some structural calculations. Engineers can do scaled drawings and can do non-structural design work. Again, the title 'engineer' is not protected and anyone using it may specialize in design for all kinds of areas, including buildings, roads or machinery. To be certain you are getting someone with the right skills and qualifications, choose someone who is a member of either the Institution of Structural Engineers (ICE) or the Association for Consultancy and Engineering (ACE).

Unqualified Designers

To check that someone calling themselves an 'architect' is genuine, contact the Architects Registration Board (www.arb.org.uk), but also look at their letterhead and company name. Someone who is misrepresenting will not state the word 'architect' on their stationery or website because this is against the law. Anyone who suggests that they have the skills and training to design and oversee the construction of a house should be carefully questioned and investigated, regardless of their formal qualifications, but if someone has none at all, a lot more questions are necessary. It may not matter to you if someone is an architect or what qualifications they have, provided that you believe that they can do the job. But if someone tries to start their working relationship with you by misrepresenting themselves as an architect when they are not on the ARB register, perhaps it is worth wondering whether they will be straight with you about other important aspects of their work.

FINDING A DESIGNER

The first stage is to draw up a shortlist of candidates, using the resources discussed below.

Personal Recommendation

This is a good way of finding an architect, but you may not necessarily come across architects in your personal or business life. Architects who do larger projects, who you may meet in your working life, may not be appropriate for a relatively small-scale project (but they might know someone who is).

The Royal Institute of British Architects

The RIBA Client Services section will give you names of local architects. However, further investigation is necessary to find out if they do your scale of project, rather than doing house-alteration work between their last factory and the next office development. RIBA Client Services can be contacted by phone or through their website, which has an online search facility (tel: 020 7307 3700; website: www.ribafind.org).

Members of the ASBA Architects' Network specialise in alterations to private houses. ASBA.

ASBA Architects

The ASBA architects' network is a non-profit-making organization that helps people to find architects who have a particular interest in the design and construction of houses, extensions, loft conversions and other associated domestic work. It has a members across the UK, all of whom are ARB registered, RIBA members and carry professional indemnity insurance. ASBA can be contacted via their website or freephone number (tel: 0800 38731; website: www.asba-architects.org).

Yellow Pages and Yell.Com

The difficulty with Yellow Pages is that all architects are listed, often with minimal information about them. A larger advert may indicate whether some of them are keen to work with private homeowners. The professional organizations usually have separate display advertisements to make their members easily identifiable. Yell.com allows a search by postcode (website: www.yell.com).

Other Projects in Progress

If you see building work going on in the area, knock on the door and ask the owners whether they would recommend the designer.

Local Authorities

Planners and building control officers should not recommend designers and builders to the public. Some may give an informal suggestion, but the ethical ones will not be keen to do so. The planning register lists names and addresses of the agents who have submitted applications recently in a district council's area, and you should also be able to see the standard of drawings that they have submitted – a reliable indication of the standard of work you are likely to get from the designer. Most planning registers are available on the council's website.

Magazines and Shows

The magazines dedicated to home alterations have plenty of illustrations and case studies of projects. The names of the design teams are usually found amongst the credits at the end of the articles. Some architects take stands at national and local exhibitions. If they have gone to the time and trouble to be there, this at least indicates they are keen to work on your sort of project.

The Internet

This is a good way to check out likely candidates' portfolios, but there are many sites that indiscriminately list practices. One of the problems is the lack of policing of the internet. Some of the listing websites allow companies to misrepresent their qualifications and do not check whether the details stated are accurate or true. For example, Google allows anyone to promote themselves under the keywords 'architects' without checking the credentials of the individuals. Although this is against the law, it is difficult to police. So if you search for 'architect', 'architectural technologist', surveyor or similar, many of the firms listed will not actually have sufficient skill and knowledge to perform these roles competently. Always check the actual experience and qualifications of anyone that you find by search engines. Unfortunately there are cases of designers borrowing illustrations from libraries or other websites to give themselves a more impressive website, so again it is important to check that the projects featured are genuine if you meet up with them.

CHOOSING THE RIGHT ONE

Once you have a shortlist of designers, and want to investigate them in more detail, there are some key things to look for, but it is your 'gut feeling' that will probably decide it in the end. Aim to meet and talk to at least two or three. If you go to more than this, they may feel it is a waste of time responding to your enquiry. The type of skilled, successful professional you are looking for may not respond to emails that have clearly been sent indiscriminately to many practices.

Interviews
Spend some time in the company of the designer under consideration. Some will be prepared to visit the site with you and make some initial comments. However, it is unreasonable to expect them to offer long consultations or several meetings without charge, particularly if your project is relatively modest. You may find that some of them will be reluctant to start giving away their best ideas until they believe that there is reasonable chance you will appoint them.

Experience
Ask how much experience the practice has had working with private clients on their homes. Are you going to be a 'fill-in' job whilst they wait for a larger, more glamorous project to come along? Do they have a good understanding of building technology, as well as having design flair? Architects used to large projects are supported by a big professional team of specialists. This is impractical for a house alteration, so the designer must be able

to handle a wide range of problems alone, as well as understanding when specialist advice is essential.

Attitude
Although the media stars of the profession can generate an impression of glamour and even arrogance, most architects are approachable, reasonable people, and would not be in business for very long if they were not. Having established that your prospective designer is in this category, you should be listening carefully to how your questions are answered. Do you get straight, clear answers? One ability, which is not included in an architect's formal training, is the ability to listen – but it is an essential characteristic for you to be able to work with them.

The Size of the Practice
Generally speaking, work on private houses is best dealt with by small- or medium-sized practices. A smaller organization will allow easy access to the directors or partners, who will at least be supervising the architect doing the work, if not producing the drawings themselves. It is a myth that experienced architects are too grand to do this kind of work. The vast majority of small practices spend most of their time working for homeowners, some of whom are only making quite modest alterations.

Previous Work
Aside from asking to see illustrations of previous jobs and talking to past clients, ask to see a set of drawings for a typical project. You may be surprised at the huge variation in the quality and quantity of drawings and specifications produced by different practices, which is a reflection of the time and care that they spend on their work. Poor-quality drawings may seem cheaper when you commission them, but the lack of skill and attention to detail can cost thousands of pounds later on in the project.

Indemnity Insurance
Registered architects have to maintain professional indemnity insurance (PII) to cover the cost of any significant mistakes that they may make. Non-architects do not have to have PII, unless they are a member of a professional organization, such

Good clear drawings help you to appreciate and visualize a design during the early stages.

existing living
room doors
kept as a
feature

N O R T H   E A S T   (B A C K)   E L E V A T I O N

For more complex projects, the architect's ability to produce 3-D visualizations is invaluable.

as the Chartered Institute of Architectural Technologists (CIAT). If a serious mistake is made that leads directly to a loss of money by their client, the insurers will pay compensation (*see* the chapter on Legal Issues for more details of PII).

APPOINTING AN ARCHITECT

Payment

Fees and charges should be discussed at an early stage. You should get a clear explanation of how fees are to be calculated, and understand exactly what level of service will be provided, as well as the payment terms, expenses charged and so on. There is a huge range in the standard of service offered. It is as important to have a fair idea of the time and expertise that will be spent on your project, as it is to know what you will be charged. A rock-bottom fee is a poor bargain if too little time is spent producing the design and drawings. Since there can easily be variations of £10,000 to £20,000 between tenders from builders, the right architect spending plenty of time on your project will easily pay for themselves.

Questions to Ask Your Designer

Are you a registered architect?
What are your professional qualifications?
How many similar projects have you worked on in the last six months?
Do you prefer to design in a particular style?
How many technical/professional staff do you have?
Who will be working on the project, and what is their experience?
Please show me examples of completed work.
How soon after receiving an instruction can you start?
How long should the project take from now to completion on site?
How are your fees calculated, and approximately how much are they likely to be?
Does the practice carry professional indemnity insurance? If so to what level?
Will there be a written contract?

Architects usually charge by the hour or a percentage of the final build cost. Which is used will depend on the level of involvement the architect is to have. At the beginning, it unwise to expect a lump sum fee, because there is no way that the time required for the design can be accurately estimated. If the architect quotes a lump sum and the job needs a lot more time than has been estimated, the project may suffer, possibly to the point that it grinds to a halt. If the architect overestimates, you will end up paying a lot more than necessary.

It is a myth that architects usually charge 10 per cent of the build cost. It will only be this much for very small or complex projects. If a partial service is required, or the project is large, or the work is very simple, it may be quite a lot less.

THE DESIGN PROCESS

Once you start work on the design, a lot of decisions will be needed to keep the project flowing along. How much you decide and how much is left to the architect will depend on your own inclinations. The design of the house should be an expression of your personality, not the architect's.

The design of a good house-alteration project must be firmly based on four basic cornerstones:

- respect for the budget,
- adherence to the client's requirements,
- practical thinking and
- an eye for what will look attractive.

This may seem common sense, but if any of these goes awry, the result is a bad design.

Typical stages for a design by an architect are:

- Set a budget.
- Discuss and agree the client's requirements.
- Measure and draw the existing building.
- Sketch out ideas.
- Discuss with the client.
- Rework design in the light of client's comments.
- Prepare planning drawings.
- Prepare construction drawings and specifications.
- Monitor the construction on site.

Checklist Menu of Services Offered by Architects and Designers

The following services are provided by most architects. If you do not require a full service, it is important to tell the architect before a fee is agreed.

Brief and Building Appraisal. A building appraisal should include a measured survey of the house and an assessment of the building's condition, as well as arranging other specialist investigations, if required. The architect will also help you prepare a brief, or list of your requirements for the project.

Sketch Design. Sketch designs consist of plans, layouts and drawings of the outside elevations. There may also be some 3-D drawings. You should be actively involved in this stage and be commenting on ideas, as they are produced.

Planning Application. It is often prudent to check with the planning department whether your design is likely to need a planning application and, if it does, whether it is likely to be approved. Planning drawings should describe the size, scale and appearance of the building work, but not the detailed construction. At this stage all the major decisions about the appearance of the finished project will have to be made.

Building Regulations. A building regulations application consists of a set of drawings, with calculations and specifications that describe the materials to be used and the basic construction of your house. Anything more than very minor building work will need a building regulations application.

Tender Package. Drawings produced to obtain building regulations' approval are totally inadequate to invite reliable tenders from builders. Giving builders detailed drawings and specifications to price from will reduce the likelihood of unforeseen overspending. The drawings should show the precise design and construction of the building and include details such as the stairs, fireplaces and the internal fittings. A specification describes the quality of both the materials and construction. The fixtures and fittings are listed in detail, covering aspects such as the manufacturer and supplier and model.

Contractors. An architect will be able to suggest reliable local builders for your tender list, invite tenders and prepare the necessary building contract documents.

On Site. If you require it, architects can act as the manager for the construction of your project. Regular visits are made to check that the works are being carried out in accordance with the contract drawings, without any unnecessary delay and in a professional, workmanlike manner.

Certificates. Architects can be used to decide how much money is due to the contractor and certify payment at regular intervals. If the work is not up to standard, you do not have to pay until the architect approves it. When the work is complete, the architect can issue a certificate and check the work six months later to ensure there are no hidden defects.

Architects are trained in construction technology and are qualified to manage a project on site, if required.

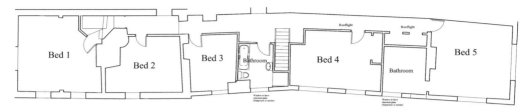

First Floor

Ground Floor

Preparation of a measured survey is one of the first tasks in the design process. The changes in wall thickness of an old property can reveal lots of information about the construction.

Once the budget and brief are agreed, the house has to be surveyed and drawings of the existing building prepared. A lot can be learnt by looking at a scaled drawing, such as a plan. A sudden increase in wall thickness may indicate that an extension has been added in the past; walls that look like they line up on the ground and first floors are found not to; design possibilities arise that were not obvious just from walking around the building. The accuracy of these survey drawings is important because they will be used as the basis for the whole of the design and detailed construction. If the design work is based on wrong dimensions, it may be impossible to build, or at least lead to some unpleasant surprises on site. A planning application can be invalidated if the planners discover the completed building is bigger, or higher or closer to a boundary than shown on the approved drawings.

The next stage usually begins with the architect developing some preliminary sketches. For a simple scheme, there may be a few possibilities or only one sensible design, in which case planning drawings can be produced quickly. If there are several options, with varying benefits and disadvantages, outline sketches may be used to examine the feasibility of each idea. Sometimes the only way to find out which concept is the best is to draw several options, only one of which will be eventually chosen. This may seem like wasted time and money, but in fact it is a lot cheaper than discovering an idea doesn't work once building work has started.

UNDERSTANDING THE DESIGN

Ideas must be described by your architect in way that you can understand. It is also necessary to illustrate ideas to others, such as planning officers and the planning committee. Two-dimensional (2-D) drawings, are a central plank in this process. Drawn to scale, they can be related directly to the building as it will be built and used as an accurate, measurable description of the finished building. However, they can sometimes be difficult to understand, or even deceptive to the untrained eye.

Two-dimensional (2-D) drawings may be adequate and cost effective for simple alterations

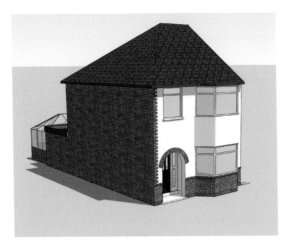

CAD model of an existing house.

The finished extension.

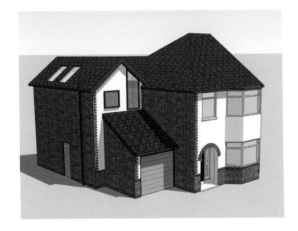

Early CAD model of the proposals.

but sometimes a design has a three-dimensional (3-D) form that may not be apparent from elevations and plans alone. Worse, 2-D illustrations may actually make such a design look unattractive. In these cases, 3-D sketches are essential. You should never approve a design unless you are confident that you fully understand it.

Cheap 3-D computer packages can be bought and mastered with some persistence, but they tend to have a limited choice of materials, components and shapes. Models can be created out of plain, white card, although this can be harder than it looks.

CREATING A DESIGN

There are many aspects that are considered as a design is being developed. Their relative importance varies according to the nature of the existing building, the taste of the homeowner and the money available. All of them offer potential clues to formulating an interesting design.

Style

You need to make an appraisal of the style of the existing house, and decide whether to keep and improve it, change it completely, or to add something new as a contrast to what is already there. The latter option is the most difficult as it needs a sensitive appraisal and response to the existing design. It takes skill to use different proportions and materials, but still produce a completed building that does not look discordant. A popular compromise is to keep an attractive traditional exterior but create a very contemporary interior design.

Contemporary Design

Older vernacular houses were built by craftsmen, using local materials and traditional building techniques. Georgian, Victorian and Edwardian buildings used the industrial technology as it became available during these periods. Today, house designers

TOP AND MIDDLE: **White-card models can be surprisingly accurate.**

BOTTOM: **A contemporary addition to a traditional house.** Acworth and Jarvis Architects.

Ten Features of a Contemporary Home Interior

- Large, open-plan spaces.
- Lots of natural light.
- Smooth surfaces with minimal details at junctions.
- Clean, straight lines.
- Monochromatic colour scheme.
- Concealed storage.
- Natural finishes.
- Industrial materials, fixtures and fittings.
- Well-designed artificial light.
- Neat, orderly lifestyle of occupants.

often plunder history for ideas. An alternative strategy is to make use of the current construction technology to design buildings that look and feel quite different to older houses.

Space Planning

It is important to be able to visualize the size and proportions of the rooms that are going to be added or altered. It is hard to do this when looking at a 2-D plan, so you may need a 3-D sketch or model. Alternatively, you relate the new spaces back to existing rooms that you know well. If the proportions of a space are wrong, it will feel uncomfortable, perhaps without you knowing the reason. We tend to relate the scale of a space back to the dimensions of our own human bodies, so that a room that is too high and narrow, or too wide with a low ceiling, will makes us feel uneasy.

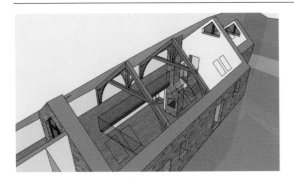

Planning is not just a two-dimensional exercise. A really creative design will use three-dimensional space.

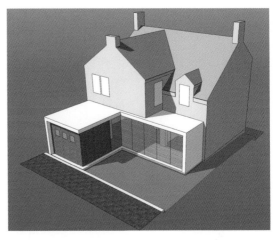

If you want to create a contrast between an existing traditional-style house and a new extension, the simplest way to do this is to use contemporary material and forms.

Structure and Construction

Traditionally built or 'vernacular' buildings were often improvised on site by their builders. Their features and appearance were dictated by the materials and techniques being used at the time. For example, the timbers used for barns and ordinary houses would not span more than about 6 metres, so this determined the maximum widths of a room and the span of a roof. With modern building techniques, method of construction of a house may be concealed or expressed. For example, some of the houses on modern estates that appear to be of solid brick are actually made from timber frame, clad in brick. Contemporary styles of building tend to make their construction a feature of the appearance.

The design of traditional houses was closely based on the construction techniques available.

Daylight and Sunlight

These free, natural resources can be used to brighten up any kind of home-alteration project. Generally speaking, the more natural daylight in a room, the more spacious it will feel. If it comes from more than one direction, quality of light is improved. The brightest source of daylight comes from roof lights. There is also a more pleasing quality that results from daylight streaming in from above.

Plenty of sunlight into a house brings many benefits, but these may be cancelled out by the overheating and glare that can result from too much sun in the summer, so buildings need to be designed so that they are oriented to avoid this problem. In the right place at the right time, sunlight will make people feel happier and may help them to be healthier.

Finishes, Colour and Materials

Some materials can be used 'self-finished', without needing to improve their appearance or weather-proofing, such as brick, stone and glass. Finishes applied to these materials rarely look good and often need frequent maintenance.

If a house is to be painted, colours should be carefully selected. The best way is to look at simi-

Sunlight is a free natural resource for
a design.

Skylights and rooflights will flood spaces
with light.

One way to make an extension look part of the original building is to render and paint it.
Left, before; and right, after.

Double-height space, lots of natural light and an interesting design make this staircase a feature of the house.

lar buildings with the treatment that you would like to use. Small swatches and samples of colours are deceptive, because the intensity of a colour is increased many times when a painted wall is compared with a small sample. What appears to be a subtle shade of rose white on a little square, turns into bright pink when spread across a whole room. As long as you are aware of this effect, a sample board can help you choose materials and finishes. It is particularly helpful when comparing different finishes, such as ironmongery and the natural wood finish of a door, or a painted architrave with the wall it will be against.

Paint can be used to bold effect, for a relatively low price, using bright colours. This can be difficult to achieve and skill is needed to avoid the end result looking garish. In some areas there is a tradition of using bright colours on render that achieves an attractive appearance to a whole street; for example, some of the Cornish seaside towns. However,

if only one house in a street is painted in this way it could look out of place, so the colours will have to be respectfully chosen.

Stairways

A staircase is often the key element in the design of a house, because it is a double-height space and is used many times a day. It should have plenty of daylight, and make full use of the change in level between the floors that it links together. If it is close by the front entrance, it will set the tone of the interior as people enter the building. Even in a modest-sized home, plenty of space around the staircase will give the whole house the impression of space. Adding rooflights and large windows can make a space feel bigger.

Front of House

First impressions count. The design of the front door and porch (if there is one) does not neces-

It is a good idea to make a design feature out of the main entrance to your house.

Traditionally we think of the fireplace as the central feature of a living room, but in reality it is the television. One solution is to combine the two.

one that it is easy to locate for strangers approaching the house for the first time. This is an opportunity to make a design statement and set the tone for the rest of the building.

Features

The careful placing of features can make an otherwise characterless room feel special. Fireplaces provide a focal point, and impose a layout on the furniture and use of a room, but an excessively large inglenook fireplace will overpower and diminish everything and everybody around it.

Landscaping

Landscaping should be considered as part of the re-design and alterations to a house. The garden can be remodelled to enhance and respond to the new internal spaces created. For example, a patio area can be integrated into a rear extension with new, full-height, glazed sliding doors, allowing you into the garden as if it were just another room.

sarily have to blend in with the rest of the house. Whatever it looks like, a well-designed entrance is

Especially for keen gardeners, the landscaping should be as much a part of the design and the extension.

CHAPTER 4

Preparing and Submitting a Planning Application

<table>
<tr><td>

What To Do at This Stage

1. Contact the Local Authority Planning Department to find out if approval is needed.
2. Obtain the Planning Officer's comments on the sketch design.
3. Amend design to take account of the Planning Officer's comments.
4. Finalize the design.
5. Check the likely cost against the budget.
6. Visit the neighbours to show them the design and get feedback.
7. Prepare and submit a planning application, by post or internet.

</td></tr>
</table>

The decision on whether or not to grant planning approval is made on behalf of a district or metropolitan council by the planning committee, which is a representative selection of local councillors. Uncontroversial decisions, especially for smaller projects, may be left to the senior planning officer, the planning committee chair and a small number of representative committee members – known as using 'delegated powers'. When there are objections to an application, especially if they are from councillors, it usually goes to the full committee for a decision. The senior planning officer makes a recommendation, but the committee may occasionally overrule him. If a councillor raises objec-

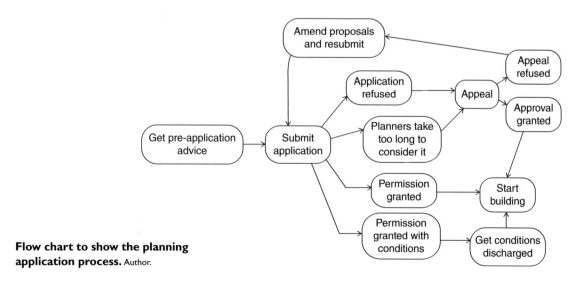

Flow chart to show the planning application process. Author.

What Happens to Your Application After Submission?

- Application checked.
- If the information is wrong or missing, the applicant is asked to put this right.
- If the fee and form are correct, the application is registered.
- Up to a seven-day wait in the 'in-tray'.
- A case officer is allocated.
- Case officer sends out consultations to other local authority officers, possibly other organizations and neighbours (for a 21-day period).
- Case officer visits the site.
- Amendments, if necessary, are negotiated with applicants.
- Case officer prepares report for the planning committee or makes a decision under delegated powers.
- Decision is made.
- Decision signed – this is the point that approval is formally granted.
- Decision letter sent.

Top Tips for Successful Planning Application

- Consult the planning office early.
- Know the local area and understand the effect and change that your project will have on the locality (if any).
- Try to be objective and keep a dialogue going with the planning officers – if there are disagreements, always be polite.
- Prepare the neighbours for the application.
- Make sure a well-presented, accurate set of drawings is submitted.
- Don't assume it will just take eight weeks – allow for delays in your programme.

tions, they are supposed to have planning-related reasons for doing so, rather than be responding to political considerations. If a councillor has become involved in the application process, or expressed views about the suitability of an application, they should abstain from voting. In reality some committee members do not fully understand their role very well and it is not unusual for them to raise objections and vote as a result of personal opinion or pressure put on them by their constituents, so committee decisions are unpredictable. If an application is approved, it is currently very difficult to get the decision reversed, but there is an automatic right of appeal against a refusal.

You can apply for either full or outline planning permission. Outline planning permission is used to test the principle of development, usually for completely new buildings, and in its simplest form, little detail is required to make up an application. If you are making significant alterations to a property or changing its use in the case of a conversion, full permission will be needed.

PERMITTED DEVELOPMENT

Unless the house is in an area of special control, such as a conservation area, householders are allowed to make minor alterations and additions without requiring formal planning approval. The list of these 'permitted development rights' is lengthy, and the local authority should always be consulted before assuming that they apply. These rights can be used only once for a house, and include any work carried out since 1948 (when the current planning legislation was enacted). So, if an extension has been added to a house by previous owners, since 1948, the permitted development rights for extensions may have been used up. In these cases you have to look at any work carried out since 1948 and add any of your new proposals to it. If this combination of alterations exceeds the allowance given by permitted development, planning permission will be needed, even if the addition is fairly trivial. Confusion can be generated by changes to the permitted development rules in 2008 – some alterations carried out before this date would not have complied under the current rights, and vice versa. If there is any doubt at all as to whether you have permitted development rights, you should check with the council and get written confirmation that you do not need planning approval before starting work.

If an extension is forward of the line of the house and facing a road, it will probably need planning approval.

For detailed guidance on the permitted development rights, refer to the later chapter on each type of house alteration.

ALTERATIONS THAT NEED PLANNING APPROVAL

It is vital to ensure that planning approval is obtained, if it is required. Should the local authority find out work has gone ahead without it, they will require you to submit an application retrospectively. If this is unsuccessful, the work will have to be demolished and the house restored to its former condition.

If a proposal exceeds the limits of the permitted development allowances, a planning application is needed. Changes of use may also require planning approval, even if there is no building work involved. For example, if you wish to use part of your home to work from occasionally, it will not usually require express permission. But if your work requires frequent visits by clients, or you start to employ people on the premises, or you make a lot of noise or cause pollution (such as excessive cooking smells or vehicle emissions), the planners consider this a 'material change' and may

require you to make an application. Usually the planners become involved as a result of complaints by neighbours.

Obtaining planning approval is the part of the project over which you have least control. You are in the hands of the local authority and whichever officer has been allocated your application, and the procedure will move at its own pace, regardless of your own wish to move forward as quickly as possible. The planning authority will consult other people and organizations, who may attempt to influence the outcome of the application. A decision should be reached within eight weeks of the application being registered, but the complexities of reconciling all the competing interests, and workload of the planning officers, mean that often it takes longer. If your proposal is particularly unusual or ignores planning restrictions, despite your best efforts, you may get a refusal and have to go to appeal, which may in turn be rejected.

IMPROVING YOUR CHANCES OF APPROVAL

There is a lot you can do to make the process of applying for planning approval less painless, but

---

Work Requiring Planning Permission

Apart from the obvious cases, the following usually need planning approval:

1. Additions or extensions to a flat or maisonette (including those converted from houses) that affect the external appearance of the building.
2. Dividing off part of the house for use as a separate, self-contained home, such as a granny flat (officially called 'dependent-relative accommodation') or bed-sit, or the use of a building in your garden as a separate residence for someone else.
3. A self-contained outbuilding in your garden with its own bedroom, kitchen and bathroom.
4. Separating off part of your home for business or commercial use (e.g. a workshop).
5. Building something that contradicts the terms of an earlier planning permission for your house; for example, a planning condition may have been imposed to stop you putting up a fence in the front garden because the house is on an 'open-plan' estate.
6. Building something that obstructs the view of road users.
7. Creating a new or wider access to a trunk or classified road.

---

never assume that approval is going to be automatic. Always allow extra time in your programme for the process to overrun the eight weeks that the local authority will quote for the consideration of an application. If you think the planning officers may not like your application, or you just want it to have a smooth passage, there is plenty that you can do to help it along.

Apart from using a good architect and paying for a well-presented set of drawings, you could employ a planning consultant. They are especially useful if the application may generate discussions about government policy, recent appeals or planning precedents, because they have a detailed and up-to-date knowledge of planning legislation.

If you think that the principle of the proposal may be a problem with the planning officers, it is sensible to get some early feedback from the planning department. If you do this, check the status and experience of the planning officer that you ask for preliminary comments. Initially you are likely to be dealing with a junior officer, who may handle the paperwork, make the site visits and so on, but the ultimate decision on whether to recommend approval will be made by someone more senior. Many local authorities now charge for this 'pre-application' advice. Unfortunately it is not uncommon for applications that are initially encouraged during these early discussions to be refused. Some-

times this is because there are some aspects of the proposal that were not obvious until either a full set of drawings was produced or a site visit was made. It might be because the initial guidance has been overruled by someone more senior, or there has been a change of officer, or that due to inexperience, the officer has simply misunderstood the council's policy. The latter happens more often than many people realize, but there is no redress that can be claimed from the council for giving misleading preliminary advice. If you are using an experienced professional to prepare the application, they may have a better idea than a junior officer as to what will ultimately be likely to be refused or approved.

Despite the problems with early advice from planning departments, it is still worth getting it, because it is certainly harder for them to refuse an application if they have previously written to

---

Hot Tip

Get confirmation of any early comments about your scheme from planners in writing. Some planning officers give ambiguous advice that might be misinterpreted as support, so carefully analyse what has been said.

---

you saying that it is likely to be approved. If you are lucky enough to get a good planning officer, it will reduce the chances of the application requiring amendments after it has been submitted. Planning departments are monitored for their speed in dealing with applications, so if they take too long it affects their overall efficiency rating. Ironically this means that if there is a relatively minor amendment needed to a design, instead of accepting a revised set of drawings, they will often ask for the application to be withdrawn and resubmitted, and threaten to refuse if this is not done. Withdrawing an application adds another eight weeks to the process for you, but this delay does not show up on the efficiency rating of the department. Knowing all this affects how you manage the application process. You need to keep 'on the case' of the planning officer and track the progress of your application – the planning office will not automatically update you with information on its status.

You should also find out whether the decision will be put before the planning committee or be dealt with under delegated powers. The latter is to your advantage if the planners are generally sympathetic, but if you feel that your application is not getting a fair hearing, you could approach some local councillors to get it put to the committee. If this still doesn't happen, more attention may be paid to your relatively minor project if it is known that councillors are taking an interest, and the planning officers will be more likely to make a balanced decision. The side-effect of rules that are designed to prevent corruption amongst local councillors is that, if one of them takes a special interest in your scheme and meets you to discuss it in detail, he or she will probably have to declare an interest and may be prevented from voting on the application. As a result, even if they want to help you, councillors will usually be wary of discussing your proposal with you without a planning officer present.

If your design is criticized by the planners, ask them to relate their comments back to their own policies and specify their concerns, rather than make standard comments. For example, if the roof is 'too high', do they mean 1m too high or 3m too high? Why is it too high? Is it because all the houses in your row are the same height, or because it will overshadow a neighbour's garden? If you know the specific problem, then re-design it lower so that it is more likely to be approved. If all they will say is that it is not 'in keeping' or it is 'incongruous', be aware that this type of general description is sometimes used by planners who just do not like something. Such language may not stand up to close analysis, particularly in areas that are a mix of different building ages, styles and design. If objections or concerns are raised by other council departments or government bodies, these should be dealt with directly, rather than through the planning officer. This saves time and avoids confusion.

Before the application is submitted, you should talk to all the neighbours who may be affected. Visit them and explain what you plan to do and why. If possible be prepared to make a few compromises if they object. If you are not able to reach a compromise, identify and address the complaints with the planning officer yourself, explaining why you think they should not prevent approval. Officially you will

Local authority planners must work to a set of rules that have been agreed democratically.
Author.

be told that objections from neighbours in themselves will not affect the chances of approval, unless they identify conflicts with the local policy that the planners have missed. In reality, an application that has strong objections from the neighbours is more likely to be refused. If there is a well-organized protest, this is very difficult to counter without going to appeal, as many local councillors will ignore planning policy and protect their chances of being re-elected by refusing, even if the officers recommend approval. When the application is eventually approved on appeal, the politicians can then claim that they have done everything possible to stop it.

If the application is going to committee, about seven days beforehand, the officers will prepare a written report and make a recommendation. If you suspect a refusal is imminent, it is useful to obtain a copy of the report before the decision is made. You may be allowed to address the planning committee immediately before the application is considered. Only do this if you are good at public speaking or can use a professional to act on your behalf. Objectors may also get the chance to put their views forward.

If you do not wish to go to appeal, but expect a refusal, it may be better to withdraw the application and resubmit at it at a later date, to allow more time for negotiations and lobbying. If an application is resubmitted within a year, you do not have to pay another planning fee for the council to reconsider it.

Although often dealt with by officers within the same department of the local authority, planning approval and approval under the building regulations are quite separate requirements, and require separate applications. Obtaining planning approval does not imply that you will get Building Regulations' approval, and vice versa.

KEY PLANNING CONCEPTS YOU SHOULD KNOW

The Local Development Framework or Local Plan

These documents state the guidelines and stand-

> **Hot Tip**
>
> Just because an unused approval has been granted in the past, it doesn't guarantee that it will get approval again after it has expired. If the planning policy has changed, it can be legitimately refused.

ards to which planning officers must work. If your proposals conflict with them, be ready for a battle, and prepare your case in advance to demonstrate good planning reasons why your application should be approved. A decision to reject an application has to be justified in the terms of the agreed planning policy and a rejection notice should state why the application contravenes it.

Permitted Development Rights

Many extensions and house alterations do not need approval if they are comparatively modest – see earlier in this chapter and the later chapter on types of alteration for more details.

Greenbelts

Greenbelts and their close relative, areas of 'open countryside', restrict development around existing towns, villages and suburbs. If a house is to be extended in a greenbelt area, planning approval may be possible, but usually anything that involves an increase in size is restricted. A typical allowance is 50 per cent by volume over and above the size of the existing house in 1948.

Conservation Areas

A Conservation Area is created where it is felt that there is a particular character or historical significance to an area that should be preserved. 'Character' is made up of streets, boundary walls and trees, as well as buildings. An 'Article 4 direction' removes the usual permitted development rights to make minor adjustments to the outside of their homes without making a formal application for approval.

If a building is listed, the alterations that you can make will be tightly controlled. The archway to this gatehouse was infilled and converted into living accommodation after permission was obtained from English Heritage and the local council.

Apart from requiring a higher standard of design and construction for any new development, the local authority may consult local history societies and other interested groups for their opinions. Many councils employ conservation officers or 'design advisors', whose job is to advise the planning officer on design matters. Assessment of design by the council frequently becomes rather subjective, as there is no way of definitively describing good design. Buildings thought of as old and ugly in the 1960s are now listed, and some award-winning designs of the late-twentieth century are condemned as eyesores by the same planners and politicians who originally approved them. Significant demolition work in a Conservation Area must be approved by the council using a process similar

to making a planning application and all sizeable trees are treated as if a Tree Preservation Order is in place.

Listed Buildings

In England and Wales, there are three official levels of listing: Grade I, Grade II* and Grade II. Grade I covers buildings of national importance, Grade II buildings of local importance and Grade II* is between the two. The main effect of listing is the restriction placed on any alterations. Grade I and II* listings usually mean that English Heritage (EH) will be consulted, whereas Grade II buildings are mainly dealt with by the local authority. Most councils also keep records of buildings that they feel are important but have failed to be listed by EH, referred to as being on the 'local list'. In theory, this has no statutory meaning, but clearly the planners will be reluctant to allow major changes to such properties.

Quite modern buildings may be listed, although if a building is over 150 years old and not significantly altered, listing is very likely. If a house is close to a listed building, the planners are likely to try to treat it as if it is in a Conservation Area. This is especially true if the proposal and listed property can be viewed together. When a building is listed, everything within its boundary is also covered, which includes relatively modern, unremarkable outbuildings, boundary walls and outbuildings. To alter any of them without consent is a criminal offence and can result in a heavy fine.

Ancient Monuments and Archaeological Areas

If the council decides that an area may have archaeological importance, it can place restrictions on any proposed building work through the planning approval process. When excavations are carried out, you may have to appoint an archaeologist to inspect holes and trenches to see whether or not there are any artefacts to be recovered or structures to record. In particularly sensitive areas, a ground investigation has to be carried out before approval is granted, usually by digging trenches or holes, as stipulated by the archaeologist. Needless to say, you have to pick up the bill for all this work.

Tree Preservation Orders

A Tree Preservation Order (TPO) restricts or prevents building work nearby that may damage a tree. Councils use TPOs to protect either individual trees, or small groups, or all the trees in a given area. They can also issue provisional TPOs very quickly, to prevent trees being felled before they are protected. Intentional damage or significant pruning is a criminal offence. The more ruthless developers know that tree protection officers are unlikely to be available over a weekend, so if there are any unprotected trees on their land that they fear may be due to be subject to a protection order, they fell them on Saturday morning.

National Parks

In these areas, the national park authority deals with most planning issues. They have a particular interest in allowing public access to the countryside, footpaths and bridleways, and the conservation of natural beauty. It is often quite difficult to justify external alterations of any type to a house. A high standard of design and construction is required, and good-quality drawings are an essential part of any application.

Areas of Outstanding Natural Beauty

These areas have similar restrictions to national parks, but are far smaller in area.

Protected Species

Certain animals are protected by law, and it is an offence to disturb them. Bats roost in derelict buildings and approval is necessary before carrying out any work that will affect them. Other creatures with this level of protection are owls, badgers, natterjack toads and crested newts. Their presence may prevent any development taking place at all, or set the time of year that work can be carried out, to avoid disturbance to breeding, migration or hibernation cycles.

Highways

If a new road access is needed, or extra parking spaces may be needed on a site, for example, because extra bedrooms mean more people and possibly more cars parked up, the Highways Officer is usually consulted by the planning officer. Highways officers will also wish to ensure that there is sufficient visibility for cars pulling out on to the road, if a new access is being created.

Controversy

A planning application should not be refused simply because the planners or some councillors personally don't like it. In reality, if you want a striking design, there may be opposition from several quarters. Unusual designs seem to be more acceptable on urban sites, but can enhance the countryside as well, if they are of sufficient quality. If you want a contemporary design, a lot of effort will be necessary to persuade both the planning officers and the local community, or ultimately a planning inspector, to accept it.

Full Planning Permission

All applications for alterations to private houses are for detailed approval, otherwise known as 'full' planning approval, and are made up of a set of drawings describing the external appearance of the proposal and plans of the internal layout.

Outline Planning Permission

Outline consent merely approves the principle of development for a particular site. Outline applications can be made up of nothing more than a set of completed forms, an Ordnance Survey map with the site outlined in red and an indication of the approximate size and location of the new work. All the details that are not shown are called Reserved Matters and need to be approved at a later date. It is unusual for this kind of application to be used for a small, domestic project, since they only prove that a type of alteration is acceptable in principle and do not give permission for an actual design.

PREPARING A PLANNING APPLICATION

Assuming that you have finalized your design and are reasonably satisfied that it has a good chance of approval, you should be ready to submit your

Checklist for a Detailed Planning Application

Covering letter.
4 sets of the completed application form.
1 certificate of ownership.
1 certificate of notification (if you do not own the site).
1 certificate of agricultural holding.
4 copies of an Ordnance Survey location plan.
4 copies of the plans and elevations.
4 copies of a site plan.
A cheque for the planning fee.

If in a conservation area, typically also:

6 rather than 4 copies of the drawings.
A design and access statement.
An application for conservation area consent if demolition is involved.

application. All the documentation has to be accurately completed, and should be carefully checked for consistency before submitting.

The Drawings

The drawings are the most important part of the application, and should be well presented and competently drawn. Poor presentation will harm the chances of approval. Inaccuracies may invalidate the approval, unless the planners notice them before the application is considered. However far you have progressed with the design, the drawings should contain as much information as necessary to obtain the approval, and no more.

A set of design drawings for a typical house will normally comprise three or four sheets of A3 paper with 1:100 scale line drawings, each clearly marked with the name of the project and given a unique number. It might not seem much in itself, but your architect will have spent a lot of time

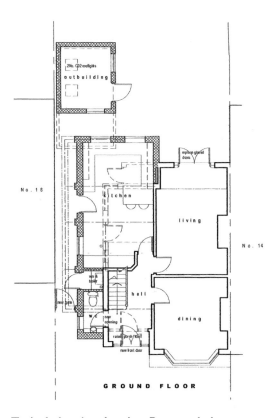

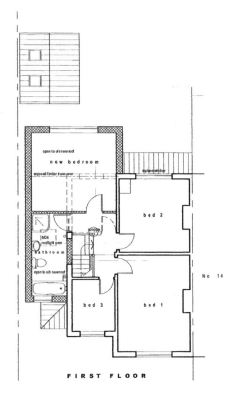

Typical planning drawing. Proposed plans.

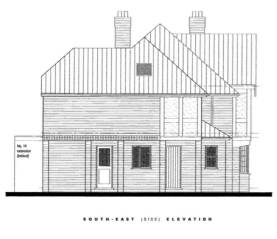

SOUTH-EAST (SIDE) ELEVATION

NORTH-EAST (FRONT) ELEVATION

Typical planning drawing. Proposed Elevations.

developing the proposals in far greater detail than is shown to the planners. It is essential to ensure that the project can be built by thinking through the later stages of the design and construction, since any alterations to the drawings after approval may require a resubmission, causing serious delay.

Extra Information

The planners sometimes ask for additional information, for example, if it is a conservation area. They may not ask for computer models, photomontages or card models in these situations, but these may be necessary to 'sell' the proposals to a sceptical planning committee. A design and access statement may be needed, which describes the thinking behind the design.

Ordnance Survey and Accuracy

An Ordnance Survey (OS) map must be included showing the location of the site and the surrounding buildings, usually to 1:1250 scale. The area of the site must be outlined on the plan in red pen, and any areas next to the site that you own or have an interest in must be edged in blue. It is essential that this map is accurate. Apart from showing the planners clearly where the site is, this drawing also defines the area that is part of the application.

Filling in the Planning Application Form

Each item on the planning application form is explained below:

1. Name and Address of Applicant. You are the applicant, in a normal situation. You don't have to own the land to submit the application. Anyone can submit an application in respect of someone else's property if they wish, provided that the owner has been notified (see Planning Certificates later).

2. Name and Address of Agent. If an architect or designer has prepared the drawings for you, it is usual for them to act as your agent. This means that any correspondence or queries go through them in the first instance.

3. Full Postal Address of the Application Site. Sometimes a property may not have a proper postal address, in which case it must be described as accurately as possible. As long as there is an OS indicating the exact boundaries, this will be acceptable.

4. Description of Proposed Development. The planners are mainly interested in the use and extent of the proposals.

5. Type of Application. You are probably asking for Full Permission – the same thing as detailed permission.

Newtown District Council

DEVELOPMENT DEPARTMENT
COUNCIL OFFICES
LETSBY AVENUE
NEWTOWN

APPLICATION FOR PLANNING PERMISSION

Application No............................
Fee Paid £ ....Rec. ....

YOU ARE ADVISED TO READ THE ACCOMPANYING NOTES BEFORE COMPLETING THIS FORM.

Four copies of this form completed in BLOCK CAPITALS, the appropriate fee and completed Certificates under Article 7 must be submitted to the above address. Cheques should be crossed and made payable to Newtown Borough Council.

1. NAME AND ADDRESS OF APPLICANT

MR H RUNE
THE MANSE
BRIGHTON
EAST SUSSEX

Post Code BN1 1AA Tel. No. 01273 121212

2. NAME AND ADDRESS OF AGENT
(If form completed by agent)

JULIAN OWEN ASSOCIATES
276 QUEENS ROAD
BEESTON NOTTINGHAM

Post Code NG9 2BD Tel. No. 0115 9229831
(Personal contact name JULIAN OWEN.)

3. FULL POSTAL ADDRESS OF THE APPLICATION SITE

THE MANSE BRIGHTON EAST SUSSEX BN1 1AA ....

4. DESCRIPTION OF PROPOSED DEVELOPMENT

GARAGE EXTENSION TO EXISTING DWELLING ....

5. TYPE OF APPLICATION - PLEASE TICK APPROPRIATE BOX

A ☐ Change of Use not involving building work

B ☑ New Building Works (Which may also include a change of use) Alterations & Extensions.

If box ticked, is application (i) FULL ☑
(ii) OUTLINE ☐

C ☐ Mining, Engineering or Other Operations

D ☐ Approval of Reserved Matters
Ref. of Outline permission ....
Date granted ....

E ☐ Removal/Variation of a Condition
Ref. of previous relevant permission
....
Date granted ....

F ☐ Renewal of Temporary Permission
Ref. of previous temporary permission
....
Date granted ....

Typical printed planning forms (there is an alternative online version of the forms at www.planningportal.gov.uk).

If you ticked 5B(ii) please answer this question

6.   OUTLINE APPLICATIONS

A   Please tick the items which are reserved for further consideration

Siting ☐   Design ☐   Means of Access ☐

☐ External Appearance   ☐ Landscaping

---

7.   SITE AREA

Please state area of application site .... 350 .... Sq. m/~~hectares~~

---

8.   EXISTING USES

Please state existing or, if vacant, the last use(s) of the site or building .... SINGLE PRIVATE DWELLING

Please tick the appropriate box

9.   DRAINAGE

	Mains sewer	Soakaway	Other
A Disposal of surface water will be to: -	☐	☑	☐

	Mains sewer	Cesspit	Septic tank	Other
B Disposal of foul sewage will be to: -	☑	☐	☐	☐

---

10.   ACCESS TO ROADS

	Yes	No
Do you intend to form a new vehicular or pedestrian access to a public road, or alter an existing one?	☐	☑

---

11.   RIGHTS OF WAY

	Yes	No
Will the proposed development affect any public rights of way?	☐	☑

---

12.   PRE-APPLICATION ADVICE

Has assistance or prior advice been sought from the local authority about this application?

Yes ☑   No ☐

If Yes, please complete the following information about the advice you were given. (This will help the authority to deal with this application more efficiently).
Please tick if the full contact details are not known, and then complete as much possible:

Officer name: MR H POOTER
Date   01.04.12
Details of the pre-application advice received:
SEE ATTACHED LETTER

---

13.   TREES AND HEDGES

Are there any trees or hedges on your own property or on adjoining properties which are within falling distance of your proposed development?

Yes ☑   No ☐

If Yes, please mark their position on a scaled plan and state the reference number of any plans or drawings:
501/03

Will any trees or hedges need to be removed or pruned in order to carry out your proposal?

Yes ☐   No ☑

If Yes, please show on your plans which trees by giving them numbers e.g. T1,T2 etc, state the reference number of the plan(s)/ drawing(s) and indicate the scale.

Typical printed planning forms (there is an alternative online version of the forms at www.planningportal.gov.uk).

14. PARKING

Will the proposed works affect existing car parking arrangements?

Yes ☑   No ☐

If Yes, please describe: NEW SPACES CREATED BY NEW GARAGE

15. AUTHORITY EMPLOYEE OR MEMBER

With respect to the Authority, I am:

(a) a member of staff   Do any of these

(b) an elected member   statements apply to you?

(c) related to a member of staff   Yes ☐   No ☑

(d) related to an elected member

If Yes, please provide details of the name, relationship and role

16. Please complete

I attach plans 501/1, 501/2, 501/3, 501/4

and I attach the completed Article 7 Certificate and the Agricultural Holdings Certificate

and I enclose the appropriate fee of £ ....150................. (see Fee List)

Signed ....*Julie C*.......................... ~~Applicant~~/Agent   Date ...01.04.12...........

CERTIFICATE OF OWNERSHIP

CERTIFICATE A

Town and Country Planning (Development Management Procedure) (England) Order 2010 Certificate under Article 12

I certify/~~The applicant certifies~~ that on the day 21 days before the date of this application nobody except myself/ the applicant was the owner *(owner is a person with a freehold interest or leasehold interest with at least 7 years left to run)* of any part of the land or building to which the application relates.

Signed - Applicant: Or signed - Agent: *Julie C*

Date: 01.04.12

AGRICULTURAL LAND DECLARATION

Town and Country Planning (Development Management Procedure) (England) Order 2010 Certificate under Article 12

Agricultural Land Declaration - You Must Complete Either A or B

None of the land to which the application relates is, or is part of, an agricultural holding.

Signed - Applicant: Or signed - Agent: *Julie Owen*

Date: 01.04.12

NOTE: Intentional misrepresentation of ownership details is a criminal offence.

Typical printed planning forms (there is an alternative online version of the forms at www.planningportal.gov.uk).

6. Outline Applications. Generally, approvals of outline applications contain a list of Reserved Matters. Not applicable to minor house alterations.
7. Site Area. This area must be defined by a red line on the location plan.
8. Existing Uses. This will tell them if you are trying to change the use of the land.
9. Drainage. The Environment Agency may be consulted if there are watercourses near to the site, which may be affected by septic tanks, etc.
10. Access to Roads. If you are creating a new drive and cross over the pavement, the local highway authority will be consulted by the planners. If a trunk road is involved, the Highways Agency, a national body, will be informed. If these organizations do not agree to your proposed new access, the application may be refused.
11. Rights of Way. If your development affects a right of way, such as a footpath, get legal advice before submitting the application.
12. Pre-Application Advice. It is usually a good idea to have consulted the planners in advance. If you do, ensure that they confirm it in writing and include this with the application.
13. Trees and Hedges. If any trees are to be felled, their location has to be plotted on the drawings. If you indicate that a tree or hedge will be removed, some local authorities automatically ask for a tree report by an arbocultural-ist, regardless of the condition or species. If they are not protected and are in the way, fell them before you make the application (assuming that they are on your land).
14. Parking. If you increase the likely occupancy of the house, e.g. by adding a bedroom, the council may require you to increase the space for on-site parking.
15. Authority Employee or Member. This is to protect the council against allegations of bias.
16. Signature. A planning application must be complete and signed before it will be accepted and logged, and a cheque for the planning fee must also be sent.

The online application process has a similar list of questions.

Planning Certificates

You also have to submit a certificate relating to the ownership and use of the land:

Part I – Land Ownership, Certificate A. You must be absolutely clear who owns all the land that forms the application, and only fill this certificate in if you are quite certain that it is you.

Part I – Land Ownership, Certificate B. If it belongs to someone else, you must send a notice to them when you submit, formally notifying them of what you are doing (not shown in the example form).

Part II – Agricultural Holdings Certificate. This is to ensure that tenant farmers and others are notified of the application. Surprisingly, if a tenant is not farming the land, rents the property on a limited lease, there is not an obligation to notify them, unless the lease is greater than seven years.

What Happens Once an Application is Submitted?

Acknowledgement
Having checked that the necessary drawings, documents and payment have all been submitted, an administration officer will log the date and time that the application is received and allocate it to a planning officer.

Consultations
Once the allocated officer has received the application, letters of notification will be sent to neighbours and other interested parties inviting comments, usually within twenty-one days.

Keeping in Touch
If you have already had a pre-application meeting or contact with the planning department, allow three to four weeks for consultations to take place before you make further contact. There may be nothing to discuss until comments are received back from the parties being consulted.

Representations

Once you do contact the planning officer, if you then find there are unanticipated problems, arrange a meeting as soon as possible. Planning departments have targets for the time it should take to get a decision made, and they will want to either get a problem sorted out, or reject the application very quickly if they don't believe that there is any possibility of a compromise.

Officer's Report

Once the planning officers have decided on a recommendation, a report will be prepared, usually recommending approval with conditions, or a refusal. In uncontroversial situations, the councillors may delegate the decision, which means that it is made by the planning staff rather than the committee.

Local Councillors

In any situation where there have been several objections, or the approval may have important implications (e.g. in a prominent location), the decision may be put to the planning committee for debate.

Planning Committee Meetings

Planning committee meetings are open to the public, and are often attended by interested parties, and journalists as observers. The officers will make their case, in a written report sent out in advance, and with a verbal summary before the application is discussed by members of the planning committee. Some committees allow short presentations from objectors and applicant. It can be helpful if a councillor speaks in support of your application.

Decision

Usually a written confirmation of the decision is sent out to the applicant and others who have made written comments within a few days. The actual approval of an application is when the decision notice is signed, not when the planning committee approve it.

Conditions

The conditions are included as part of the Approval Notice and are integral to the permission. Some

> **Hot Tip**
>
> Make sure if you use an agent that you obtain the original approval document for your records. It is a legal document and may be required when the house is sold.

are fairly standard; for example, requiring that the brick and tile samples have to be approved by the Council. Others can cause expense or may be less acceptable; for example, a requirement to provide space for more cars on the site. Conditions that could add to the cost include mining and contaminated land reports and tree reports. If you think a condition is unreasonable, or unenforceable, you can appeal against it in a similar way to a refusal of planning consent, but you must do this promptly.

Appeals

If you get a refusal, you can resubmit an amended application, if you can accommodate the modifications required. If you are unable to do so, you can go to appeal. If you do this, it is essential to get some professional advice, either from your architect or a planning consultant. Appeals are decided by a government-appointed inspector who is from outside the area. The appeal may be dealt with in writing only, at a private hearing or in public. An excellent booklet on how the appeal process works is published by the Planning Inspectorate and is available from your local planning office.

SUMMARY

At the end of the planning process, you will have an approval document to carry out your alterations. Very minor changes can be agreed as amendments to the application, but major variations, such as an increase in height of an extension, would require a fresh application. The process from submission of the application to getting approval should take about eight weeks, but if you hit problems, it can take twice as long. Work must start on site within three years, after which time the permission usually expires.

CHAPTER 5

Preparing and Submitting a Building Regulations Application

Planning permission is not the only approval needed from the local authority. You may also need to get approval under the building regulations. Although usually administered by the same council department, it is a completely separate process, involving different officers. Granting of planning approval does not imply that a design will get building regulations' approval, and vice versa. Whoever prepares the planning application must also be very familiar with the regulations, to ensure that there is no conflict. Unlike the planning process, you do not have to employ a local authority building control officer to check and approve your scheme under the building regulations. You can go to an approved inspector, using private companies that provide this service – although they still have

to keep the local authority informed of what they are doing for you. In the past, approved inspectors tended to be quicker and more accommodating than local authority officers, although in recent times the latter have been taking a more commercial approach and provide a more efficient service.

WHAT ARE THE BUILDING REGULATIONS?

The building regulations ensure that all significant building work complies with minimum standards of construction. They protect the health and safety of those who use or live in a building, now and in the

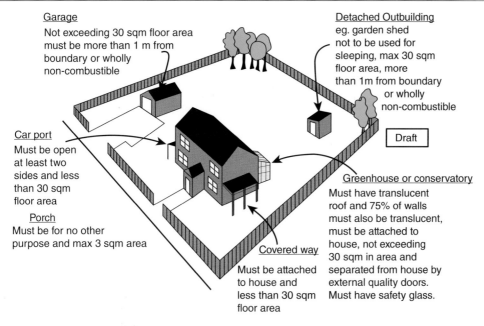

Garage
Not exceeding 30 sqm floor area must be more than 1 m from boundary or wholly non-combustible

Detached Outbuilding
eg. garden shed not to be used for sleeping, max 30 sqm floor area, more than 1m from boundary or wholly non-combustible

Draft

Car port
Must be open at least two sides and less than 30 sqm floor area

Porch
Must be for no other purpose and max 3 sqm area

Covered way
Must be attached to house and less than 30 sqm floor area

Greenhouse or conservatory
Must have translucent roof and 75% of walls must also be translucent, must be attached to house, not exceeding 30 sqm in area and separated from house by external quality doors. Must have safety glass.

Some alterations and extensions do not require approval under the building regulations. Author.

future, by checking that the construction is sound. They also protect the interests of the general community as well. An example of this is the requirement for energy efficiency and to reduce the amount of carbon that buildings put in to the atmosphere over their lives. The primary legislation passed by Parliament, states that a building must comply with these overall requirements, but detailed guidance is given in a set of booklets called 'Approved Documents' (ADs), which are regularly updated to keep up with good practice.

Because the ADs change regularly, designers and builders have to ensure that they keep up do date. If you can prove that there are other ways, not shown in the ADs, that still comply with the law, which could be summed up as 'it should be built properly', you don't have to follow their detailed guidance. However, unless you are innovating in some way, the simplest course of action is to follow the suggestions in the ADs.

Obtaining building regulations approval is relatively straightforward, compared to getting planning approval. The regulations are generally very clear as to what has to be done, and building control officers are pragmatic people, who will agree to changes on site provided that they are happy that the regulations are being complied with in principle.

Ultimately it is up to you, the person commissioning the building work, to ensure that building work complies with the regulations. You can delegate a main contractor or site manager to do all the work for you, but from the point of view of the regulations, the buck stops with the homeowner.

In a similar way to permitted development rights, which effectively exempt some alterations from requiring planning approval, there are many apparently minor building works that in fact need approval under the building regulations. These include:

- Fitting new windows in new openings or replacing existing windows.
- Fitting out a bathroom, where the appliances are in new locations.
- Creating a new opening in a structural wall.
- Fitting a new boiler, even if the rest of the system is not altered.

- Installing cavity insulation.
- Replacing a flat roof with a new, pitched roof.
- Converting a garage to a room, even if there are no structural alterations.
- Changing the use of a building, e.g. converting two flats into a single house.
- Replacing the covering of a pitched roof with a different material.
- Altering or installing a new ring main.

FULL PLANS APPROVAL

There are three ways of getting approval under the regulations and completing work to a house. The safest procedure involves two steps. Drawings and specifications describing the basic construction of the building are submitted with a fee. The application is for 'full plans approval'. After two or three weeks, a building control officer or approved inspector writes to whoever has submitted the plans, asking for any amendments or extra information. Once this is provided satisfactorily, 'full plans approval' is granted, in the form of an approval notice. Quite often, approval will be conditional on further information that is not currently available being provided; for example, roof truss calculations, which will only be provided by a supplier once an order is placed, long after construction has started.

The approval process usually takes between four and six weeks to come through after submission, and you can then start work on site after giving a couple of days notice. You can start work fairly confident that the house will comply with all the major requirements of the regulations, and have some drawings that can be used as a basis for its construction. If an approved inspector is used as opposed to the local authority, the full plans process can be fast-tracked and issued within days, if necessary, usually subject to a long list of conditions.

Full plans approval does not guarantee that the finished building will comply with the regulations. It is simply a check that all the major requirements of the regulations have been considered and incorporated into the design. Once work starts on site, building control officers do not have to check the quality of workmanship or the standard of finishes. Their only obligation is to see that the work complies with the regulations.

If the builder follows the approved drawing and specifications, and agrees any changes with the building control officer, you can be confident that the building will comply once completed. The building control officer will make inspections at pre-agreed key points in the programme. On completion you should get a certificate confirming that the house has been built in accordance with the regulations – essential when you come to sell the property later. A fee is paid when the plans are submitted, about 25 per cent of the total, with the balance being paid once work starts.

BUILDING NOTICE

If a project is very straightforward or involves a standard design that has already been approved, you can use the building notice procedure. A short form is completed, 48 hours before work starts, and sent in along with a fee. No detailed drawings or specifications are prepared, and the builder works without them. The building control officer or approved inspector makes site visits to check the work as it progresses. This route is unsuitable for anything other than very simple projects. An experienced builder is needed to carry out the work because if anything is built that does not comply with the regulations and it is not noticed until later on, the inspector will require the work to be taken down and rebuilt. The project will suffer delay and extra cost if this happens. The fee to serve a building notice is the same as for the full plans approval route, but instead of being paid in two stages, it is all due when the notice is sent.

Hot Tip

Drawings prepared just for a building regulations application are not suitable to get fixed-price quotes from builders. A lot more detail is needed to work out an accurate cost.

REGULARISATION CERTIFICATE

A lot of work is carried out to private houses and on commercial buildings without seeking the necessary building regulations approval; this is illegal. It often happens due to ignorance, but occasionally because the client or contractor wishes to avoid the extra cost. If the regulations are avoided wilfully and the case is serious, the local authority can prosecute and get the offender fined many thousands of pounds. What is more likely to happen is that on discovery you will have to ask for building regulations approval to be applied retrospectively, by applying for a Regularisation Certificate. If you are in this unfortunate situation you will be required to uncover any work that has been concealed as a result of the work being finished, to demonstrate that it complies with all regulations. This opening up could cause extensive damage; for example, if the floorboards have to be lifted, or plasterboard taken down.

Local authorities rarely pursue cases of minor building work built without approval, mostly because they don't find out about them. The commonest reason that Regularisation Certificates are applied for is when a house is being sold. The purchaser's solicitor asks to see a copy of the building regulations approval certificate and the vendor has to correct the omission before the house can be sold.

The building regulations are described in a set of 'Approved Documents' that each deal with a particular aspect of building construction. Author.

the regulations, preferring a more flexible system based on guidance contained in techincal handbooks. The handbook for houses has six sections, covering structure, fire, environment, safety, noise and energy, and is accompanied by a procedural handbook and a certification handbook. Approval can be obtained from an 'approved certifier', who issues certificates to the local authority as evidence that the regulations have been complied with. The whole system is administered and monitored by the Scottish Building Standards Agency.

ENGLAND AND WALES vs SCOTLAND

The procedure covered in this book mainly relates to the building regulations as they apply in England and Wales. Scotland has significant differences. North of the border, work cannot start until a building warrant has been issued (you can start before plans approval has been granted in England and Wales, if you wish). Also, in Scotland a new house cannot be occupied unless a habitation certificate has been issued at the end of the project. In Northern Ireland, the rules are very similar to England and Wales.

The Scottish regulations shy away from stipulating constructions and details that comply with

APPROVED DOCUMENTS (ADs)

The approved documents go through each aspect of building construction and give detailed advice on how to meet the legal requirements. At their best they are very clear, and contain useful construction details. At their worst, they list complicated calculations and confusing cross-references that require real expertise to interpret. Copies can be ordered from most bookshops, and can also be downloaded free from the government's website. Anyone who is going to carry out significant building work must first be familiar with the relevant ADs.

Even a well-prepared, detailed set of plans will not cover every regulation. Many of the regula-

The Approved Documents of the Building Regulations

A. Structure
B. Fire Safety
C. Site Preparation and Resistance to Moisture
D. Toxic Substances
E. Resistance to Passage of Sound
F. Ventilation
G. Hygiene
H. Drainage and Waste Disposal
J. Combustion Appliances and Fuel Storage
K. Protection From Falling, Collision and Impact
L. Conservation of Fuel and Power.
M. Access and Facilities for Disabled People
N. Glazing – Safety in relation to Impact, Opening and Cleaning.
P. Electrical Safety

Note: there is no Document O.

tions are assumed to apply, or may be covered with phrases such as 'drains to be laid in accordance with Approved Document H of the Building Regulations'. The purpose of the full plans approval is to identify compliance of the major aspects of the construction, not list every last paragraph from the approved documents. Consequently, no one should work on your project unless they have a basic knowledge of the approved documents. Much of the guidance covers non-domestic buildings and is irrelevant, but each of the ADs has something in them that affects the way that houses are planned and built.

One anomaly is that most of the building regulations do not apply to external works, beyond the access from the road and the area immediately around the house.

Building regulations application drawings have to describe the basic construction of the proposed building work.

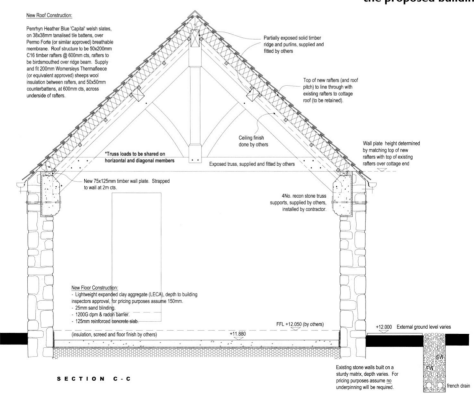

New Roof Construction:

Penrhyn Heather Blue 'Capital' welsh slates, on 38x38mm tanalised tile battens, over Permo Forte (or similar approved) breathable membrane. Roof structure to be 50x200mm C16 timber rafters @ 600mm cts, rafters to be birdsmouthed over ridge beam. Supply and fit 200mm Womersleys Thermafleece (or equivalent approved) sheeps wool insulation between rafters, and 50x50mm counterbattens, at 600mm cts, across underside of rafters.

Partially exposed solid timber ridge and purlins, supplied and fitted by others

Top of new rafters (and roof pitch) to line through with existing rafters to cottage roof (to be retained).

Ceiling finish done by others

*Truss loads to be shared on horizontal and diagonal members

Exposed truss, supplied and fitted by others

Wall plate height determined by matching top of new rafters with top of existing rafters over cottage end

New 75x125mm timber wall plate. Strapped to wall at 2m cts.

4No. recon stone truss supports, supplied by others, installed by contractor.

New Floor Construction:
- Lightweight expanded clay aggregate (LECA), depth to building inspectors approval, for pricing purposes assume 150mm.
- 25mm sand blinding.
- 1200G dpm & radon barrier.
- 125mm reinforced concrete slab.

(insulation, screed and floor finish by others)

+11.880

FFL +12.050 (by others)

+12.000   External ground level varies

Existing stone walls built on a sturdy matrix, depth varies. For pricing purposes assume no underpinning will be required.

SW
FW
french drain

SECTION C-C

MAKING A BUILDING REGULATIONS APPLICATION

Drawings and Specifications

If you are using an architect to prepare a tender package as well as to obtain building regulations approval, the same set of drawings and specifications can be used for both. If, to save money on the architect's fee, you have asked for 'building regulations only', this is probably what you will get – just enough information to get full plans approval and no more. These drawings do not need to be particularly detailed, and will not tackle many of the day-to-day construction problems, which will have to be sorted out on site. The largest scale needed is 1:50, which does not really tell you much about the detailed construction, other than the broad principles, which is all the building control officer is looking for at this stage.

Hot Tip

Building regulations-only drawings are relatively quick to prepare and seem cheaper than a full tender package. But once on site, the builder may ask for extra payment to work out missing details or change those that don't work well because they have not been explained or resolved.

Structural Calculations

Approved Document A is about making sure that the building will stay up, and bear the loads and stresses that are put upon the structure comfortably. To prove that the structure is sound, calculations have to be prepared, usually by a structural engineer. These calculations may cover aspects such as adequacy of the foundations for a given type of soil, the size of beams and the stability of walls. Once submitted, they are checked by another engineer, on behalf of the local authority or approved inspector.

Filling in the Form

The application form is short, and only requires the main details about the project. The questions to pay special attention to are:

Item 5. You should always agree to conditional approval. Otherwise the application may be refused unless everything has been approved, even though the information may not be available straight away. If approval is granted conditional on further information being submitted later, it must be approved before the relevant work is carried out.

Item 6. It is sensible to agree to an extension of time to the prescribed period. Like their planning colleagues, building control officers are under pressure to deal with applications promptly, so if they run out of time and you won't agree to extend it, they may issue a rejection notice.

Item 7. A house is not covered by most of the fire regulations, beyond those listed in the approved documents.

Item 8. It is essential that a completion certificate is requested as part of the full plans application. If it not, there may not be an obligation for one to be issued, but it is a vital document to have when the house is sold.

WORKING WITH BUILDING CONTROL OFFICERS AND APPROVED INSPECTORS

After a full plans application has been submitted, the building control officer will usually have some

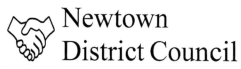

Newtown District Council

DEVELOPMENT DEPARTMENT
COUNCIL OFFICES
LETSBY AVENUE
NEWTOWN

Application No................................
Fee Paid £ ....Rec. ....

A typical building regulations application form.

Building Regulations
Full Plans application

Receipt No. . . . .

Notice of intention to erect, extend, or alter a building, execute works or install fittings or make a material change of use of an existing building.
I/We hereby give notice of intention to carry out the work set out herein in accordance with the accompanying plans.

Signed . . . .   Date . . . .

1.	NAME AND ADDRESS OF APPLICANT	2.	NAME AND ADDRESS OF AGENT (if applicable)

1. NAME AND ADDRESS OF APPLICANT

MR HUGO RUNE
THE MANSE
BRIGHTON
EAST SUSSEX

Post Code BN1 IAA... Tel. No. 01273 121212

2. NAME AND ADDRESS OF AGENT (if applicable)

JULIAN OWEN ASSOCIATES
276 QUEENS ROAD
BEESTON NOTTINGHAM

Post Code NG9 2BD...... Tel. No. 0115 9229831
(Personal contact name JULIAN OWEN......)

3. FULL POSTAL ADDRESS OF THE APPLICATION SITE

THE MANSE, BRIGHTON, EAST SUSSEX BN1 IAA

4. DESCRIPTION OF PROPOSED DEVELOPMENT

GARAGE EXTENSION TO EXISTING DWELLING

5. CONDITIONS Do you consent to the plans being passed subject to conditions where appropriate? YES/NO
6. EXTENSION OF TIME If it is not possible to give a determination within the prescribed period do you consent to an extension of time? YES/NO
7. Is the building to be put to a Designated Use for the purpose of the Fire Precautions Act? YES/NO
8. Do you wish to receive a Completion Certificate on completion of the work? YES/NO
9. Is a new vehicular crossing over the footway required? YES/NO
10. Means of water supply MAINS
11. Details and dates of any additions made to the property since 1948 (this includes garage, conservatory, etc.). NONE
12. State whether building is private, Council or ex Council PRIVATE
13. Amount of fee enclosed herewith £ 100
14. Fee payable for inspection of work £ 250
15. Estimated total cost of work £ 30,000
16. Floor area of proposal Sq. m 60

This form must be accompanied by two sets of plans and the appropriate fee.
Where Part B (Fire Safety) applies a further two sets of plans are required.

questions, or require extra information, before the plans are approved. Surprisingly, similar applications to different local authorities, or even different officers, result in a different set of queries. Approved inspectors are usually more open to negotiation as to how much is needed before they will issue an approval. This checking process can be invaluable because it helps to ensure that any potential problems are picked up and dealt with at an early stage. Likewise, a competent officer inspecting a site provides an extra pair of eyes working on your behalf.

Site Inspections
The inspecting officer must be informed, and the inspection fee paid, at least two days before work starts on site. There follows a series of inspections at the most critical points in the building

programme. The latter officially require at least one day's notice, but local authorities and approved inspectors usually start work early and carry out office administration duties up until around 10.00am, after which they will set off to carry out their inspections. So, provided a builder telephones early enough, a site meeting can be set up the same day.

The building control officer/approved inspector's duty is to ensure that the building regulations are being complied with and nothing more. They do not provide a quality control service or monitor the progress of the builder. A helpful building control officer will make informal comments, off the record, but many do not have the time or inclination to get involved beyond their statutory duties. If a brick wall is structurally sound, its appearance is not their concern, not even if it is patchy because the pallets of brickwork have not been mixed up after delivery. Likewise, if the specification or design has been changed by the builder without asking you,

Building control officers make periodic visits to site to check that the work complies with the regulations.

Typical Building Control Inspection Stages

Inspections will broadly follow the list shown here, but if a building control officer knows, and has confidence in, the builder, there may be fewer inspections than if there are concerns.

Commencement (two days' notice).
Foundation trenches dug but not filled.
Foundations filled with concrete.
Subfloor ready, concrete slab about to be laid.
Concrete slab laid.
Damp-proof course level achieved.
Fixing of floor timbers.
Fixing of roof timbers.
Drains – laid but excavations not backfilled.
Drains testing.
Occupation (if not yet compete).
Completion (two days' notice).
Certificate of compliance issued.

All the above require one day's notice, except where stated otherwise.

as long as it still complies, there is no onus on the building control officer to point this out.

Many approved inspectors and building control sections offer an extended service, where they will go beyond the simple checking of the regulations and offer a building guarantee or certificate that can be used to satisfy lenders or future purchasers.

WHAT CAN GO WRONG?

If you make a full plans application, the chance of something going wrong is greatly reduced, and the problems on site are unlikely to be complex. Occasionally, something proposed, or even built, does not meet with the approval of the building control officer.

Problems at Full Plans Stage

If something is wrong on the plans, the first review of the applications should pick it up, and it can be easily discussed with the architect and corrected – assuming that the revisions do not affect the planning approval. A classic case of the building regulations clashing with the planner's requirements is the need to add a new opening window at first-floor level, with a sill low enough to allow a person to escape if there is a fire – but if it would look out over the neighbour's garden, the planner would be unlikely to allow it.

Unlike a planning application, rejection of a full plans application is not as bad as it sounds. If you resubmit the amendments straight away, most of the checking will have already been done and the approval can come through in a matter of days.

Failure to Comply On Site

If something is built that does not follow the approved drawings and specifications, or that was not described by them, and the building control officer decides that it is contrary to the building regulations, you will have to demolish it and rebuild. The building control officer can halt and condemn work if you try to ignore any direction to correct a contravention. There is an appeals process, where you ask for the government to decide if the rules have been correctly interpreted or should be relaxed in your case. Such a course of action will be protracted and result in considerable cost and delay to the programme.

SPEEDING UP THE PROCESS

Ideally you should wait for planning approval, then have a building regulations package prepared, then a tender package and then appoint a contractor. This takes time, but it is the safest way to proceed and will greatly reduce the risk of work having to be redone. But if speed is essential, there are ways to reduce the time needed to get work started on site. Work can start on the building regulations drawings before planning approval is granted and completed by the time the decision notice arrives. You may be fairly confident of getting planning approval, but it is not unusual for planners to ask for any amendments or alterations to even a modest scheme. If a shortcut is taken, any changes

that result from the planning process will require the more detailed building regulations drawings to be amended, at extra cost.

Another way to save time is to start on site two days after the building regulations application for full plans approval has been submitted. This procedure is used for fast-track commercial projects and is fine, provided you are totally confident that any work carried out during the first few weeks of building will definitely comply. Your architect is unlikely to guarantee this because the consequences of being wrong can be very expensive, so it would be your risk. This condensed timetable is still a better option than the highest risk route – that is serving a building notice without any drawings at all. If you have submitted a full plans application, the checking process will eventually catch up with the building work, and you will get warning of any problems at that point.

A compromise is to wait until the inspector comes back with initial enquiries following the full plans submission before starting to build. This should at least indicate the areas that are questionable. If none of the queries involves the early stages of construction, it should be safe to start on site. Unfortunately, the structural calculations often take longer than anything else. There is an obvious risk in carrying out any structural work before approval is in place.

SUMMARY

To get approval under the building regulations, all your designer and builder have to do is comply with the approved documents. Anything not in the ADs does not need to be checked for compliance. Aspects of your project, such as decorations and fittings and fixtures, are of no direct interest to the building control officer or approved inspector. So, a building regulations package is not sufficient on its own to fully describe what is going to be built. Many more decisions have to be made, either by the architect preparing a tender package or by you, or the builder or a tradesman, or a bricklayer on site, as he wields his trowel. It is your choice which of these applies.

CHAPTER 6

Key Facts for Home-Alteration Projects

LOFT CONVERSIONS

Loft conversions are a popular choice of alteration, particularly in areas where land is expensive and gardens are small, ruling out ordinary extensions. With the right type of roof construction, they are fairly straightforward and usually relatively quick to build.

An Ideal Loft Conversion

There are a number of features that will make a loft easier to convert. The larger the area with clear headroom there is in the existing space, the better. The only way to assess this is to climb into the loft, stand up in the middle and use a bit of imagi-nation while checking some basic dimensions. The area that is above head height before the conver-sion will be reduced by the alterations that will have to be carried out. As a rule of thumb you can add about 50mm to the existing rafter depth and 50–75mm to the floor height. The narrow strip of space under the ridge that has clear headroom is the starting point for space planning. The wider this area is, the easier it will be to plan. A gable roof will provide more area than a hipped roof, and may also be possible to fit normal windows into the walls at each end.

If the existing joists are designed only to support the ceiling, they will not be strong enough to support the loads imposed by bedroom use,

---

Is a Loft Conversion Right for Your House?

- 400mm to 500mm is needed above your head when you stand up in the existing roof space.
- The fewer alterations to the structure of the roof, the easier and cheaper the conversion is likely to be. Trussed rafter roofs, where there are many sections of timber criss-crossing the roofspace, need special treatment.
- The roofspace should be large enough to accommodate at least a bed, some furniture and possi-bly an en suite bathroom.
- If the current roofspace is not large enough, it must be possible to extend it, e.g. by adding dormer windows.
- A proper staircase up to the new space will have to be constructed and 2m headroom must be achieved above each tread, but especially at the top.
- If there is not sufficient headroom over the stairs, a dormer or similar extension to the roof will be necessary.
- The occupants of the loft space must be able to escape safely in the event of a fire.

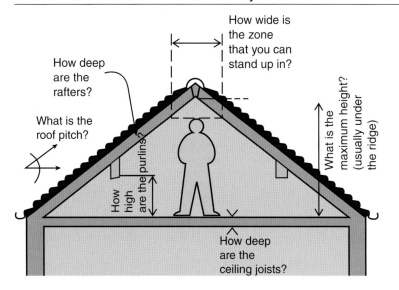

How deep are the rafters?

What is the roof pitch?

How wide is the zone that you can stand up in?

How high are the purlins?

What is the maximum height? (usually under the ridge)

How deep are the ceiling joists?

What to look for when considering converting a loft. Author.

so deeper floor joists will have to be installed in between them. If the ceiling joists are already quite deep, the new structural floor level may not have to be a lot higher, but will at least need to be boarded out with floorboards or chipboard, adding an extra 22mm or so. If there are purlins (horizontal beams that the rafters rest upon), it is better if they are either high enough to be above any new windows, or lower than the 1,100mm maximum window-sill height required by the building regulations. Otherwise, it will be necessary to cut them and introduce any new structural beams and props.

An ideal loft conversion will have plenty of headroom, a staircase that is more generous than the minimum required by building regulations and plenty of space.

Many loft conversions benefit from the addition of dormer windows. They create more space with

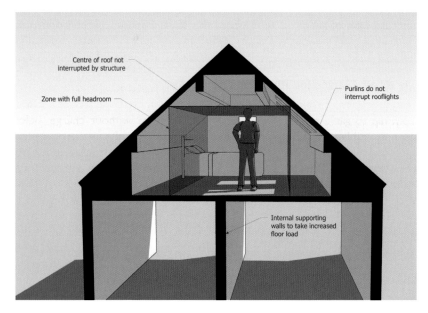

Centre of roof not interrupted by structure

Zone with full headroom

Purlins do not interrupt rooflights

Internal supporting walls to take increased floor load

An ideal, simple loft-conversion. Author.

headroom and add interest to the interior room. In some cases they are essential to make a conversion possible.

Planning Permission and Loft Conversions

Quite often, loft conversions do not need planning approval. This is because most of the alteration work is inside the building and not visible. The rules for allowing alterations to the outside without needing express planning permission – known as 'permitted development rights' – are sufficient to cover many typical types of conversion.

Permitted Development Rights
Assuming that your house is not in an area of special control, you are allowed to make alterations to the roof without applying for planning approval, as long as it complies with the following requirements:

- The volume added is no greater than 40m³ for terraced houses.
- The volume added is no greater than 50m³ for detached and semi-detached houses.
- No extension is to be built beyond the plane of the existing roof slope of the principal elevation that fronts the highway.
- No extension is to be higher than the highest part of the roof.
- Any materials used are similar in appearance to the existing house.
- No verandas, balconies or raised platforms are to be built.
- Side-facing windows have obscure-glazing, with any side-facing opening 1.7m above the floor.
- Roof extensions, apart from hip to gable ones, to be set back, as far as practicable, at least 200mm from the eaves.
- Roof extensions are not permitted developments in designated areas, such as conservation areas.

Building Regulations for Loft Conversions

The building regulations are more onerous for rooms that are higher than one storey above ground, so some of the rules that apply to the loft

A dormer window under construction. It will allow more headroom in the roofspace.

conversion of a two-storey house do not apply to the conversion of a bungalow roof.

Information on how to comply with the building regulations in the England and Wales is published by the government in a series of booklets, called Approved Documents, and there are similar standards published in Scotland for building warrants. These can be bought in printed version or obtained on government websites without charge. Below are the key regulations that affect loft conversions in England and Wales, with some exceptions for bungalow roof-conversions.

Building Regulations Approved
Document A – Structural Stability
The guidelines contained in Approved Document A ensure that any building work carried out is structurally safe. They will usually require the ceiling joists to be strengthened to take the floor loading that will be imposed from furniture such as

beds and bookcases. A particular issue is when the beams supporting the rafters, known as purlins, are cut through, to allow the roof space to be enlarged. The regulations require that this kind of alteration to the main roof structure is examined by an engineer or similarly qualified professional, who has to produce structural calculations to show that the new structure will be strong enough to satisfy the regulations.

Building Regulations Approved Document B – Fire Protection, Spread and Escape

The aim of the regulations is to ensure that anyone using the loft space has enough time to escape safely if there is a fire. The higher the building, the harder it is to get out quickly, so the rules are not particularly onerous if the loft being converted is in a bungalow, where it is possible to climb out of a first-floor window to escape. However, once you are up above first-floor level, it becomes much more important that the occupants of the loft rooms get clear warning when a fire starts, and then have time to escape before the stairwell becomes impassable due to smoke and heat. Failing that, the loft needs to be safe enough for people to remain in until rescue arrives. Incidentally, the escape rules are not aimed only at loft conversions, many of them also apply to houses with three full storeys or more.

Escape from a Loft Conversion Added to a Two-Storey House

If a conversion is added to a two-storey house, a protected escape route is created from the loft down the stairs and all the way to the outside of the building. The walls around this escape route usually have to last for at least thirty minutes and the doors for twenty minutes before the fire and smoke starts to get past them. In other words, anyone in the loft will be guaranteed at least twenty minutes within which to realize that there is a fire and escape from the building without being exposed to flames, heat or smoke at a life-threatening level. New constructions can easily be built to comply with these requirements, using standard stud partitions, with 12.5mm plasterboard, or ordinary masonry walls. Older constructions, such

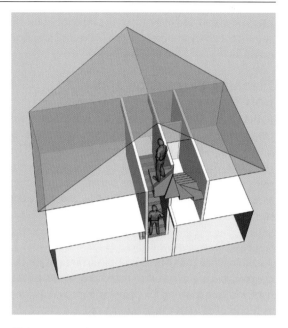

If the new staircase does not lead to a hallway that in turn leads directly to the outside, escape routes in two directions through existing rooms will satisfy the regulations. Author.

as existing lath and plaster walls, are unlikely to achieve the required thirty minutes and will have to be upgraded by covering with plasterboard.

New fire-resisting doors are readily available. The existing doors all along the escape route have to be replaced or upgraded to resist fire for twenty minutes, a standard referred to in the regulations as FD20 or E20. 'FD' stands for 'Fire Door' and is a UK standard and 'E' stands for 'Europe', but there is no real difference between the two. Some types of door, especially the older panelled ones, are difficult or impossible to upgrade and have to be replaced. Hinges have to be steel, and special seals between the door and frame that expand when they get hot may be needed (known as intumescent seals). The ceiling between the loft and the rooms below may also have to be upgraded, to provide thirty minutes' fire-resisting construction. This means that for thirty minutes it has to remain strong enough to stand on, stay intact and insulate the rooms above from the heat. For a small loft-conversion it is possible to get this requirement relaxed and expert help is advisable if this is necessary.

If the intention is to comply with the regulations by providing a single escape staircase with a thirty-minute protected route all the way down and directly to the outside, all the bedrooms in the loft have to open directly on to the stairwell and it must be possible to get from the bottom of the ground-floor staircase to an outside door, without going into another room.

A common problem with this approach to complying with the regulations is that in some houses, the bottom of the staircase on the ground floor opens into a room, rather than a hallway leading to an outside door. This is considered a risk to people trying to escape. There are several ways of dealing with this. Many older houses, particularly those that started their life as the 'two-up two-down' variety, have the staircase in the centre of the building to save space, with the front door opening into the front room. It may be impractical to create a protected corridor from the bottom of the stairs to the front or back door, because the room that it passes through is too small or windows will be lost. The regulations allow an alternative solution, which is to provide two escape routes in different directions and through different rooms. However, to comply to the regulations with this approach, the bottom of the staircase must be enclosed in the fire-protected walls and have fire doors leading from the stairs into each room.

In some modern house layouts, the bottom of the staircase is directly into a living room, with no hope of arranging an alternative direction of escape. In these circumstances, the regulations can be satisfied by adding a fire door at the top of the staircase on the first floor, ensuring that the ceiling between ground and first floors is fire-protected to thirty minutes and an escape window at first-floor level. To be classified as an 'escape window'

the window must comply with the regulations (see the section below on bungalows and extension later on in this chapter for more details). The open-plan ground floor must also have a water sprinkler system added. The idea is that in the event of a fire, people can get to first-floor level safely and then escape through a window.

Smoke alarms are required on every floor. Usually one in the hallway and one on each landing are sufficient, although it is advisable to have them fitted throughout the house at the same time. Ordinary battery-operated smoke alarms are inadequate for the regulations because they can fail unless regularly maintained. Also they will only sound once the smoke has reached them, so if someone is asleep in the loft, they may not hear a ground floor alarm two floors away. The regulations require mains-operated alarms, on a separate circuit, linked together, so that if one goes off the others will also be activated.

Escape from a Loft Conversion Added to a Bungalow
The requirements for conversion of a bungalow's loft are less onerous than for a two-storey house because it is easier to escape out of the loft windows, which are only at first-floor height. The simplest method of providing escape is to open the rooms off a new staircase up from the ground floor

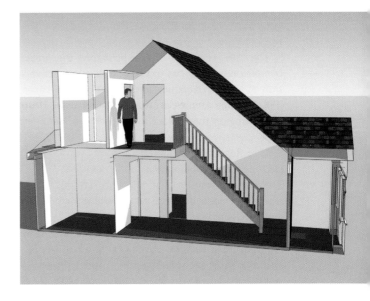

The best arrangement for a new staircase in a bungalow is for it to lead up from the main hallway. Author.

hall, which does not have to be a fire-protected exit, and ensure that the new windows to the loft comply with the regulation requirements for escape windows.

If it is not possible to fit escape windows to the loft, perhaps because of planning restrictions that prevent windows overlooking neighbours, the alternative is to upgrade the staircase to thirty-minute fire-resistance and have an exit to the outside or in two directions. If even this is not practical, it may be possible to provide a separate external escape staircase and upgrade the ground-floor ceiling to provide thirty minutes' fire protection, which is also permitted by the regulations.

Escape from a Loft Conversion Added to a House with Three Storeys

Complying with the regulations to escape from the roof space of a house with a second floor or higher can get more complicated. The most straight-forward way is to upgrade the staircase to be a protected route, either with an exit to the outside, or in two directions on the ground floor, or allow escape from the first floor with similar provisions to the two-storey house scenario described above. If the existing stair cannot be upgraded, the provision of an advanced fire-detection and alarm system is a possible route to complying with the regulations, although this has to be in conjunction with either a separate fire-escape stair or the installation of a sprinkler system throughout the whole house.

The fire regulations are probably the most complex issue that has to be tackled in the conversion of a loft. In anything but the simplest of cases, it is advisable to seek professional guidance before embarking on the project.

Building Regulations Approved Document E – Sound Insulation

These rules require that adequate sound insulation is provided between the new rooms created and between new and existing rooms. The requirements for floor construction can usually be met by incorporating 100mm of mineral wool insulation into the gaps between the floor joists. Masonry walls, particularly brick, will probably comply if they are lined with plasterboard or covered with two-coat plaster finish. Stud walls can be made to comply either by doubling up the plasterboard on each side or, if there is only a single layer, by adding 25mm or so of mineral wool into the gaps between the studs.

Approved Document K – Staircase Design

Very occasionally, the restrictions placed by the regulations on staircase design can make a loft conversion impossible to achieve. More often they make the conversion difficult, requiring accurate measurement of the existing spaces and careful

A common location for a staircase to a loft conversion over a semi-detached house is directly over the existing staircase. A new dormer window is needed to ensure there is enough headroom (minimum headroom is indicated in red). Author.

design. Usually, the designer is trying to keep the staircase as compact as possible, because it takes space away from the areas of the loft with good headroom as well as from the floor below.

The staircase must not be too steep. There is an absolute limit on the height of the each step up or 'riser' on the staircase, and a minimum length for the spacing between each riser, known as the 'going'. The rules say that the rise shall be between 155mm and 220mm, which can be used with any going between 245mm and 260mm. There is an additional provision that twice the rise plus the going should be between 550mm and 700mm (2R + G = 550 – 700mm). In addition, there is a maximum angle or 'pitch' allowed for the whole staircase and minimum headroom of 2m required in most cases. Where the staircase steps go around a corner, with triangular treads known as 'winders', the turn must not be too tight and cramped.

A special exemption to these otherwise strict rules has been created for loft conversions, known as an 'alternating tread' stair. This is steeper than a normal staircase, but it saves space by providing the length of going needed only on one side of each step. To go up the stairs you always have to start with the same foot (either left or right) and go up placing a foot on the side that has the right size of tread. It is allowed in private houses because the assumption is that the occupant will come to know how to use the staircase well and will not get it wrong, even in the middle of night when they are half asleep. If someone unfamiliar with such a staircase tried to use it, especially in the dark, there is a risk of falling. An alternating tread staircase is not recommended for use by the elderly or partially infirm.

The headroom requirements are designed to allow everyone, except the unusually tall, to walk up the stairs without bumping their head. The requirement for at least 2m above the run of the staircase that applies to new staircases in all houses is again relaxed slightly in recognition of how difficult it can be to achieve for a loft conversion.

Approved Document L1 – Insulation and Heating
This document is designed to minimize the heat loss from the building, partly to save the occu-

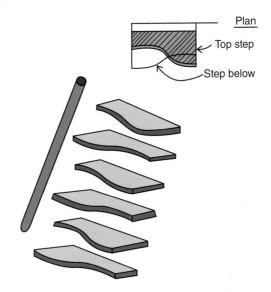

An alternating-tread staircase. Author.

pants' money on their heating bills, and partly to reduce wasted energy and carbon dioxide emissions into the atmosphere (the main culprit causing global warming). A typical specification that will satisfy the requirements, at the time of writing, is 100mm of high value insulation between the rafters with 40mm fitted across and underneath them. However, the provisions to reduce energy usage are now revised every three years or so and are becoming increasingly stringent.

EXTENSIONS

Although they may add considerable value to a house, extensions may not always cover their full costs but they are often cost-effective compared to moving house.

Apart from the obvious functional role of adding more room to the house, an extension may also significantly affect the appearance. It should integrate well with the existing floor-plan and be straightforward to maintain. If the new addition fails to satisfy these requirements, it will detract from your home and, in extreme cases, reduce its value. On the other hand, a skilfully designed

The left-hand side of this house has been extended, with the material and design carefully chosen to match in with the original house on the right.

extension can be used to transform the way that a house looks and feels, and help to make a previously unlovable property desirable.

When it comes to deciding the approach to the design, there are two alternatives: either the design matches in with the proportions and materials of the existing building, or you contrast new with old and create something that is quite different. Whichever route you choose can be made a success. The worst approach is to ignore the influences of the existing building altogether, which usually produces an unsatisfactory and unattractive result.

Matching the new work in closely with the existing building is usually the easiest option, particularly from the point of view of planning officers and committees who rarely reward boldness when it comes to house alterations. But doing this properly is not always quite as easy as it sounds. Traditional houses use timber floor joists that cannot span further than about 6m, and so room sizes tend to reflect this limitation. Clay tiles hang at an angle of at least 35 degrees and are prone to being lifted by

the wind if they are any shallower. These limitations are not imposed by modern building methods and the free availability of technology, such as rolled steel joists (RSJs) with their greatly increased spans and concrete interlocking tiles that can be laid in large slabs at angles as low as 15 degrees. The latter allows a large single-storey extension to be added to the rear of a house, but it will never look part of a traditional-looking original building with such a shallow pitch.

Adding something with a more contemporary flavour needs a carefully planned approach to ensure success. You will need an architect with design flair and ideas will have to be presented with skill, since it is harder for planners, neighbours and councillors to visualize more modern designs from basic drawings. The normal standard two-dimensional elevations drawn for a traditional design often make a contemporary addition look deceptively ugly, because it has been designed in three dimensions and needs to be seen like that for it to make sense. Consequently, computer-generated or white-card models may be necessary for the designer to convince you and others that the end result will be attractive. If an extension is small enough to be within permitted development rights (see below), it can be more radical and it is quite hard for planners to prevent it from being built (although not impossible, because they can insist that the new material matches the existing (see item 12 of the list of permitted development rights below).

Planning Approval and Extensions

Ground-floor extensions to the rear of houses are rarely controversial when it comes to obtaining planning approval. This is because the main pre-occupation of planners is the impact that will be made on the surrounding neighbours. If you wish to add to the first floor and above, it attracts more scrutiny. However, the permitted development rules allow you to add quite a bit to the original house before you need to make a planning application.

Permitted Development Rights

An extension or addition to your home will not require a planning application, provided it is within the following limits and conditions:

1. No more than half the area of land around the 'original house' would be covered by additions or other buildings.
2. No extension to be forward of the principal elevation or side elevation fronting a highway.
3. No extension to be higher than the highest part of the roof.
4. The maximum depth of a single-storey rear extension is 3m for an attached house or 4m for a detached house.
5. The maximum height of a single-storey rear extension is 4m.
6. The maximum depth in plan of a rear extension of more than one storey is 3m, including the ground floor.
7. The maximum eaves height of an extension within 2m of the boundary is 3m.
8. The maximum eaves and ridge height of the extension must be no higher than the existing house.

9. Side extensions must be single storey with maximum height of 4m and width of no more than half the original house.
10. Two-storey extensions to be no closer than 7m from the rear boundary.
11. The roof pitch of extensions higher than one storey must match the existing house.
12. Materials must be similar in appearance to the existing house.
13. No verandas, balconies or raised platforms are included.
14. The upper-floor and side-facing windows to be obscure-glazed (i.e. glass that allows light through but not a view and usually has a patterned or irregular surface); any openings must be 1.7m above the floor.
15. On designated land there is no permitted development for rear extensions of more than one storey.
16. On designated land no cladding of the exterior is permitted development.
17. On designated land no side extensions are permitted development.

'Designated land' usually means in a conservation area, an area of outstanding natural beauty, national park or similar protected land. These permitted rights do not allow alterations to listed buildings – listed building consent is required for any alterations. The term 'original house' means the house as it was first built or as it stood on 1 July 1948 (if it was built before that date). Although you may not have built an extension to the house, a previous owner may have done so.

If you do need to apply for planning approval for your extension, there are some rules of thumb that most local authorities apply when assessing the application, which it is worth knowing before anyone starts drawing up a design.

Overshadowing and Overlooking

If the new addition gives you a prominent view directly into your neighbour's garden, or into their windows that are close to the boundary, this will cause some concern for the planners. They will also assess whether significant daylight is lost to the neighbours' ground-floor windows by a new

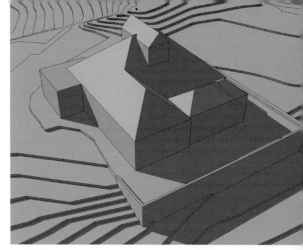

Existing house plan. If a property is far enough away from a public road, the permitted development rules allow sizeable additions.

section of first floor. In many cases, especially urban and suburban areas, an extension to one house is bound to have a noticeable effect on its immediate neighbours. What the planners have to do is decide whether that effect is significant; in their language whether it is 'detrimental to the amenity' of the neighbouring properties. Making this assessment can be quite subjective – in many cases the neighbours object to anything that has any effect at all on their property. But a neighbour objecting is not grounds for a refusal of permission.

To help them make consistent decisions, most local authorities use a combination of 'rules of thumb' and written policy. They often have writ-

ten in to their development policy set distances that must be achieved between the different types of elevation of houses. For example, the fronts of houses may have to be at least 22m apart and the side of one house may have to have 15m between it and a rear elevation of another house. Another favourite is to set the minimum depth of a back garden at 10m. These rules are mainly for new housing estates, but they will usually influence the assessment of applications for extensions to existing properties. Unfortunately, they vary between councils, so you have to check with your local authority to find out what they are for your house, and how rigorously they will be applied.

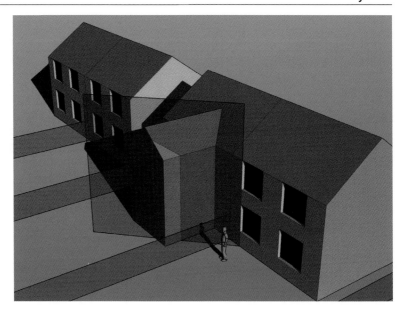

To prevent overshadowing, the planners draw an imaginary 45-degree line from the side of your neighbour's window. In this case, the area of the proposed first-floor extension beyond the red plane would probably be refused. Author.

A classic 'rule of thumb' used by planners to decide whether to allow a first-floor extension to the rear of a house, is to draw a 45 degree line in plan from the edge of the neighbour's closest ground floor window across the back of your garden. If the proposed extension crosses this line it will be at risk of being rejected.

The problem with applying these general rules is that sometimes they are not appropriate or do not apply to a particular situation; for example, where there is a steep level change between the houses. It can sometimes be a challenge to get planning officers to accept this and make a decision that goes against the grain.

Relationship to Adjoining Buildings
When planners use the well-worn phrase 'in keeping', they are asking for the new addition to match not just the materials of the surrounding buildings, but also, in theory, their size, scale and proportion. They also prefer extensions that are visible from the road to be 'subsidiary' to the existing house. In effect, the ridge height of the new building is expected to be lower than the main ridge height. The latter can be difficult to achieve if a large addition of floor space is needed at first-floor level, and also illogical if the house can be made to look

better by adding something of a similar size that matches in well with the original, so negotiation is needed in these circumstances.

Another phobia of planners is called the 'terrace effect'. The thinking goes that if you have a typical suburban street, made up of rows of semi-detached houses and they all decide to add extensions close up to their side boundaries, the street will then look like a terrace of houses. This is considered a bad thing, and the solution is to insist that any such extensions step the first floor back from the front face of the house. The street will then look like a row of terraced houses with the first floors close to the boundary stepped in, which is considered a good thing. This rule of thumb seems to be applied ruthlessly throughout the UK. The only difference is the distance that is considered an acceptable indent. Some insist on 2m, others will tolerate 1m. If it is far enough from the boundary, building the extension wall flush with the existing front wall may then be acceptable.

Building Lines
It is not unusual, particularly in older housing estates, for the front faces of the buildings to be in line with each other. Less planned roads also tend to have stretches of houses that are approximately

Existing house before extending at the side.

House with new extension added to the right-hand side. Planners will typically ask for a setback at first-floor level to avoid the 'terrace effect'.

aligned. This is referred to as the 'building line' and again any new extensions that are proposed that are nearer the road than their neighbours are considered to be a potential threat to the quality of life, order and harmony of the neighbourhood. If it can be shown that there is a building line along the road, and that your proposal breaches it, your application will be refused.

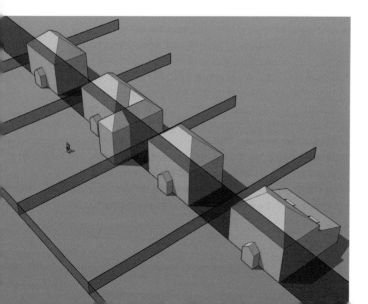

Building Regulations for Extensions

Although all the regulations apply to extensions, there are one or two aspects that are particularly worth noting.

Building Regulations Approved Document B – Fire Protection, Spread and Escape

In a normal two-storey house, the regulations stipulate that some of the upstairs windows should be wide enough and low enough for someone to climb out if there is a fire. These are called 'emergency egress windows'. One of these is required in all habitable rooms upstairs and also on the ground floor if the room does not open directly to the outside or to the hallway. A 'habitable room' is a

If there is a building line at the front of a row of houses, the planners are unlikely to allow a two-storey extension to project beyond it. The proposed extension second from the left falls into this category. Author.

A window suitable to escape from in the event of a fire, according to the building regulations. Author.

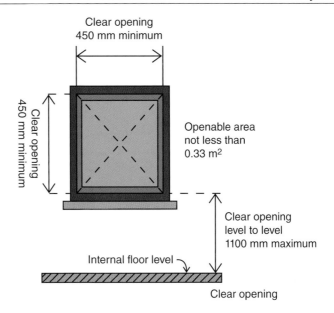

Clear opening 450 mm minimum

Clear opening 450 mm minimum

Openable area not less than 0.33 m²

Clear opening level to level 1100 mm maximum

Internal floor level

Clear opening

bedroom or somewhere you are likely to be in for a while, but not rooms such as bathrooms or cupboards. Many standard windows comply with the minimum size requirements, but sometimes the lower window sill is an inconvenience; for example, in rooms-in-the-roof in bungalows, where the roof pitch makes it quite hard to achieve. If a house has three floors, it has to have a protected fire-escape stairwell, removing the need for emergency egress windows for all rooms that lead off it.

Planning departments often limit the size and location of windows close to, and facing, the boundary and building control officers also have restrictions. The latter is because, if a house catches fire, it can spread between properties through windows close to a shared boundary. So the size and number of windows in an extension wall, close to a boundary, are restricted, particularly if the new wall is closer than 1m. Another regulation that affects windows is the requirement to provide fresh air to a room. The regulations say that sufficient fresh air is available if the total area of openable window in a room is 20 per cent the size of the floor area. There is a potential conflict between these two regulations – one limiting the size of window, the other requiring it to be larger, that can be resolved only by introducing mechanical ventilation.

A garage is considered a potential source of fire, because of the petrol in the fuel tank of cars, so there has to be at least thirty minutes' fire-protection between the garage and the rest of the house. The regulations also consider the risk of spilt petrol flowing under any doors into the house, and require a step up from the garage to prevent this.

Approved Document L1 – Insulation and Heating
The rules controlling how much energy is needed to heat new additions to a house are far more demanding than the time when global warming was not recognized as a problem. Regardless of how well or badly the existing house is insulated, the new roof, walls and floor must be up to current standards. If the area of glass minus the area of existing openings covered up by the new building work is greater than 25 per cent of the floor area, then a calculation is necessary to show that the heat loss from the whole of the house, after it has been extended, complies with the regulations. It follows from this that if you intend to increase the area of glass beyond the 25 per cent figure, you will have to increase the insulation levels of the new walls, and possibly add insulation to the existing walls, to compensate for the heat lost through the glazing. The calculations that are needed are

relatively complex and usually carried out by a specialist using computer software.

CONSERVATORIES

Conservatories are a popular type of home improvement. When a conservatory is well sited and intelligently designed, it can be an asset to a home by providing a light, airy room that has a quality quite different to a normal extension made from a solid roof and walls. Unfortunately there are many occasions when the addition of a conservatory has blighted a property rather than improved it. The main reason for this is that many conservatories are sold using high-pressure sales techniques that are more to do with gaining a commission rather than giving homeowners good advice. The objective of the poor salesman is to get you to agree to something quickly, without thinking too much about it or talking to alternative suppliers. Never buy a conservatory without getting several other quotes and satisfying yourself that you are getting a fair deal. There are plenty of decent conservatory suppliers, who will offer you a good product that is designed and built to a high standard. It is worth taking the trouble actively to find this kind of firm and invest the extra money they will charge, because their work will enhance the value of your house. A poorly designed, wrongly positioned, badly built conservatory makes your house worth less than before it was added.

Good conservatory suppliers will discuss your project with you, survey your house and then suggest a design that will match your budget and property. Finding the right supplier means following the same principles that apply to finding a general builder, but one thing to look for is FENSA registration. The Fenestration Self-Assessment Scheme allows qualifying companies that register with them to avoid the need for another party to check that they have complied with the relevant building regulations when fitting doors and windows.

Conservatories are usually bought as a standard design with the supplier also constructing it. Some suppliers do not carry out the related building work, such as digging the foundations and building the low-level brick walls. Others will carry out

this work, but add the cost on as an extra to the advertised price. A reliable building contractor may be able to negotiate a better price for you with a conservatory supplier and still make himself a profit.

The most important consideration affecting comfort for the occupants of a conservatory is how it relates to the sun. The heat produced by sunlight gets trapped behind glass – the 'greenhouse effect'. As soon as the sun shines on a conservatory it starts to warm up. If it faces south, directly into the sun, it can heat up to over 38°C (100°F) in the summer, unless something is done to reduce it. Levels over about 25°C are uncomfortable, so a south-facing conservatory in summer is an unpleasant place to be. It will only be at a tolerable temperature for about two hours in the morning of a sunny day before the heat starts to build up.

Although it traps heat from the sun due to the greenhouse effect in summer, glass is not very good at retaining heat in winter because it is a poor insulant. Even when facing south, the solar gain from the sun is not enough to make a difference if the

---

Key Facts for Conservatories

- Never site a conservatory on a south-facing wall unless there is plenty of shade from trees – it will be too hot in summer and too cool in winter.
- Blinds are an attractive feature and will screen direct sunlight, but will not completely prevent the heat build-up in direct sunlight.
- To help air circulation and cooling in the summer, all conservatories should have openable windows at low level, as well as at high level in the roof.
- Conservatories are a very quick way to extend your home and a single room-sized structure can be fitted by a competent DIY enthusiast.
- The planning requirements that apply are the same as for normal extensions.
- Most small conservatories do not require approval under the building regulations.
- A cheap, badly sited conservatory will reduce the value of a house.

outside air is very cold, so the conservatory will be too cool most of the time – below the 17°C minimum that we need to be comfortable. In fact, if a conservatory is positioned on a north-facing wall, over a typical year it is at an acceptable temperature for more hours in the day than if it was to face south. This is because, although a north-facing

conservatory is unusable in winter, so is a south-facing one most of the time. However, in summer, the north-facing conservatory is sheltered from the fierce sunlight and so remains cooler and more pleasant.

So in most cases it is a very bad idea to locate a conservatory on the south wall of your house.

Typical Tricks Used by Unscrupulous Salesmen to Sell Conservatories

- At the end of a month they tell you that they need to sell just one more conservatory to hit their sales target, so will offer it to you at a 'special price'. However, you have to agree to buy straightaway, otherwise it will not count towards their target. In most of these cases, the only thing special about the price is that it is high and they don't want you to shop around and find this out.
- At the beginning of the month, they tell you that they want to get their sales off to a good start and so for today only they are offering a special price, provided you agree straightaway. As above, the special price may in fact be inflated.
- In the middle of negotiations, they tell you that the price you are suggesting is so low they are not authorized to agree to it and they will have to phone their boss. The boss at the other end of the line always seems to agree to the bargain, provided you sign straightaway.
- They offer you a lower price for a conservatory that is the end of a line, or is from a sale that has fallen through, or is ex-display. As usual, you have to agree immediately before someone else snaps up this unique offer.
- They offer to introduce you to another company that will arrange the finance for you. If investigated closely, you might find that the loan offered is highly uncompetitive compared with a normal high street bank – and that a large commission goes to the salesmen for persuading you to sign up for it.

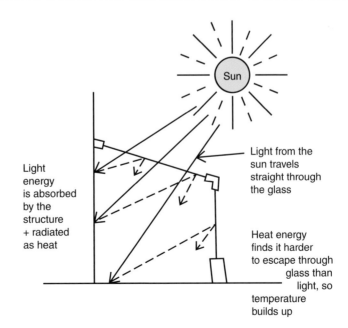

The greenhouse effect means that south-facing conservatories get unbearably hot. Author.

Light energy is absorbed by the structure + radiated as heat

Light from the sun travels straight through the glass

Heat energy finds it harder to escape through glass than light, so temperature builds up

Blinds and ventilation can help to reduce the over-heating in summer to a certain extent, but they do not solve the fundamental problem.

Planning Permission for Conservatories

The planning system treats conservatories just like any other type of extension, so the rules covering permitted development, conservation areas and so on, all apply in the same way. Consequently, because by definition they are only ground-floor extensions, most small conservatories are unlikely to require express planning permission.

Building Regulations for Conservatories

It is not necessary for building regulations approval to be sought for most conservatories because, in contrast to the planning rules, they are treated as a special case. Provided that they are within the following limits, they can be built without needing inspections from a building control officer or approved inspector:

- The construction meets the definition of a conservatory under the regulations, i.e. the roof is 75 per cent translucent and the walls are 50 per cent translucent (excluding existing walls).
- It is for domestic use only.
- It is single storey and at ground level.
- It is not used as a bedroom.
- There are no alterations to the existing drainage system.
- If the conservatory has heating, it must be possible to switch it off independently from the rest of the house.
- Any doors between the conservatory and the rest of the house are of external quality.
- The total floor area of the conservatory is less than 30m^2.

This does not mean that none of the regulations apply. Document N, which deals with safety glass, must be complied with. However, the requirements for limiting heat loss stated in Document L, which would be impossible to satisfy with an extension that is mostly glazed, do not apply.

BASEMENTS

Many houses have existing cellars that may possibly be converted into habitable rooms. In areas where there is no space to go up or out, the construction of a completely new basement under a house may be an option, but the land values in the area must be very high to justify this as an investment. The expensive option of excavating a new basement can only be cost-effective in expensive areas such as central London. The other key factor in the success of a new or converted basement is the ground conditions. Well-drained subsoil, such as sandstone, well above the water table is best. Impervious ground, such as heavy clay or with a high water table, may make a basement impractical.

The addition of a basement to a home will only be successful if its uses are considered carefully. Most basements are completely underground and,

Key Facts for Basements

- Is there an existing, unconverted basement already under the house? This is usually much cheaper to convert, compared to an entirely new excavation.
- If the ground conditions are poor, e.g. heavy clay or high water table, creating a basement for normal use may not be a realistic option.
- Basements are excellent for some uses, such as TV rooms, games rooms, gym, utility room and storage.
- They usually have little or no natural light or ventilation and so basements do not make good bedrooms and living rooms.
- Safe escape from a basement in the event of a fire in the rooms above is essential.
- As a general rule, if it is possible to add extra space to a house above ground (e.g. a normal extension), this is a better investment than creating a basement.
- Once a basement has been created and made watertight, the other main problems to be solved are providing good-quality light and supplying adequate ventilation.

A typical use for a basement is for a swimming pool.

if there are no windows to the outside, mechanical ventilation and artificial lighting become essential, making use for bedrooms or a lounge difficult. Conversely, allowing natural light and ventilation will broaden the range of possibilities. This can be done easily if there is a difference in level between the front and rear of the house because a pleasant room can be created, even if only one side has a view and an openable window. If the external levels around the house are only just below the ground floor level of the house, there may still be ways of improving the quality of the new rooms. Provided the garden is large enough, a lightwell can be created or even a whole patio area at basement level. Alternatively, it may be possible to cut away some of the internal ground floor to allow light to filter through from the ground floor windows, particularly in the area of a staircase.

Toilets, showers and bathrooms are possible in a basement, but because they will usually be below the level of the main drains, a pump is usually necessary. There are plenty of proprietary pumps, designed for exactly this purpose that work well. The only downside is that they make a little more noise than a normal toilet flushing.

Expanding and upgrading an existing cellar is more cost effective than the creation of a completely new basement under the house. A new basement is likely to cost twice as much as upgrading a cellar. There are many factors that will affect the level of building work needed, mainly related to the construction and location of the existing house, but the major costs usually result from making the building envelope properly watertight and creating a strong construction to resist the loads that result from the ground that bear on to the walls. An existing unused basement, typical of late-Victorian terraced houses, may have no waterproofing and have a low ceiling height. These are not a problem if the space is used for storage, coal or similar, but means it cannot be used for habitable rooms without significant alteration work.

Waterproofing a Basement
The level of waterproofing needed partly depends on the ground conditions. If there is a high water table, or the ground is poorly drained (e.g. heavy clay), there will be water pressure on the walls – in other words, it is similar to the basement being built in a lake, surrounded by water pressing to get

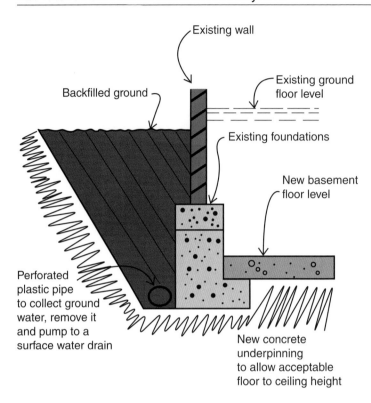

Existing wall

Backfilled ground

Existing ground floor level

Existing foundations

New basement floor level

Perforated plastic pipe to collect ground water, remove it and pump to a surface water drain

New concrete underpinning to allow acceptable floor to ceiling height

Creating a new basement under an existing house. Author.

low level at all times, to prevent the air from becoming damp.

Structural Work for Basements

Where an existing basement has a low ceiling, the extra height needed is gained by excavating down. Usually the walls stop at the existing basement-floor level, so they have to be extended down, by a process called underpinning. This is where a wide, solid wall of concrete is built under the existing foundations, down to just below the new floor level. If there is no basement at all and a completely new one is being created, the underpinning starts immediately below the ground-floor walls and is consequently more extensive. If the underpin-

in. These conditions need extensive precautions to prevent water getting to the internal spaces.

The simplest method to deal with the risk of damp is to line the internal walls with a water-proofing sheet, or render. This is the cheapest way of applying waterproofing. However, if there is any actual water pressure on the walls from the outside, it will push its way through and dislodge the waterproofing layer. The second method relies on the construction itself being a barrier. Ordinary bricks or blocks cannot do this, but reinforced structural concrete can because it is almost impervious, except at its joints. The third method assumes that significant moisture will get through the construction and creates a cavity in the wall for it to run down. At the bottom of this cavity any water that builds up is collected into a drain and pumped away. None of these methods prevents all moisture from finding its way into the room, which is why mechanical ventilation should be run at a

ning has to be quite deep, it will need reinforcing with steel to strengthen it against the dead weight of the subsoil that pushes upon it. Underpinning is a specialist job and needs experienced builders to carry it out. How easy it is depends partly on how much space there is around the house and how easily the builder can gain access to the walls. The worst case is for a terraced house, where access under the external walls has to be through the house, rather than from the outside. If the house is a terrace or is semi-detached, the Party Wall Act will apply and the correct procedure will have to be followed, with notices served on the relevant neighbours (see later chapter).

Planning Permission for Basements

Lowering the floor of an existing basement below an ordinary house should not require planning approval, assuming that there are no extensions or alterations that impact significantly on the out-side (especially at the front). Whether or not a completely new basement needs planning permission is, surprisingly, a grey area that has not been totally resolved in the UK at the time of writing. When the current revisions of the permitted development rules were published in October 2008, they made no specific reference to basements. This has now been recognized as a mistake, because it leaves the question of the need for planning approval in doubt. Some local authorities interpret the permitted development rules that allow a house to be extended as also applying to basements. This means that, provided those restrictions on size and height are followed, basement conversions that are wholly under the house are permitted development. However, this view is not universal and some planning departments have interpreted the silence regarding basements in the permitted development rules as meaning that they will always require planning approval.

A proposal to create a new category of permitted development that deals with basements has been made by the government, but not implemented. So it is essential to consult your local planning department to find out whether they think it needs a planning application and if so, whether they are likely to approve one.

Building Regulations Approval for Basements

Most basement conversions and all newly-formed basements require approval under the building regulations. If it has existed and is being used as a habitable space, not all the regulations will apply, because you are improving an existing situation. If a new basement is being created under a house, all the relevant regulations may be enforced. Some of the regulations that are particularly worth noting are given below.

Building Regulations Approved Document A –
Structural Stability
The basement construction will have to hold back

the weight of subsoil pressing on the walls. In poorly drained areas, there will be water building up and bearing on the walls as well. It is essential that a qualified structural engineer is involved in the design of the construction and the building control officer will insist on it.

Building Regulations Approved Document C –
Resistance to Contaminants and Moisture
The most relevant sections of this document relate to waterproofing and structure, and are strictly the province of experienced construction professionals.

Building Regulations Approved Document B –
Fire Protection, Spread and Escape
It must be possible to escape easily in the event of fire, and the regulations state minimum requirements that are necessary to achieve this. The simplest way to satisfy them is to provide an alternative escape to the staircase, in the form of a window or, ideally, a door to the outside. If this is not possible, a fire-protected stair that leads to the outside, rather than through another room, should be provided. All new steelwork should be fire protected.

Approved Document L1 – Insulation and Heating
Both the floor and walls of new basements must be properly insulated. The level required is calculated by a series of charts and tables that are not easily summarized, but are based on the depth of the basement, the area of the walls and floor and the length of the perimeter.

Approved Document F – Ventilation
Because most waterproofing systems are not 100 per cent impervious to moisture, a small amount will get through into the rooms below ground, raising the humidity of the air. The regulations recognize this and require that some form of artificial ventilation is used, unless natural cross-ventilation using windows is possible. Even if there is little moisture present, it is essential for health to have fresh air circulating around the basement.

CHAPTER 7

Being Green – Sustainable Construction

Sustainable construction is the current buzzword for what is also called 'green' or 'environmentally friendly' building. It means that when any building work is designed and carried out, the impact that is made on the environment is considered. This is an issue that has rightly been increasing in importance over recent years. Our homes are amongst the worst offenders, responsible for about 25 per cent of all carbon dioxide emissions in the UK. Carbon dioxide causes global warming, which is going to have a detrimental impact on our lives as it progresses. But even if you don't believe this, one absolute certainty is that fossil fuels are dwindling and will become more expensive in the future. So if you intend to live in the house for many years after the alterations are complete, it makes good economic sense to consider ways of reducing the energy demands of the house.

The aspects of the UK building regulations that affect sustainable design are gradually being made more strict and prescriptive, and there is no doubt that this will initially make it more expensive to alter an existing dwelling. You would have to be able to charge a premium for the extra energy efficiency of the house to get your money back when you sell it, which does not tend to be possible at the moment. One possibility is for the energy provider (e.g. electricity supplier) to lend the money to cover the cost of the work. The idea is that they then recover the repayments on the loan by adding it to the greatly reduced quarterly bill. In other words, the repayments are made by whoever

owns the property. It is possible that by 2016 many new types of design and construction methods will have to be employed just to comply with the regulations. At the moment, the regulations are not so onerous that they will have a serious impact on

Underfloor heating can be energy efficient if it is combined with the right heating system.

the cost-effectiveness of a project, but many people have an ethical commitment to saving energy and causing less harm to the planet with their lifestyle. If you are in this category, you will want to think quite carefully about the influence this approach will have on the initial cost.

It is a potentially vast subject and if you are interested in pursuing sustainable ideals, it is well worth getting one of the many books that describe in depth how to be as 'green' as possible when building. One problem is that some of them offer conflicting advice, and there are not always clear-cut answers as to the best way to achieve an environmentally friendly house. Because of the huge growth in interest in sustainable construction, and perhaps also because many people like to be seen to be making their own personal contribution to reducing global warming, there has been a rise in the availability of 'eco-bling'. This term covers components and products that imply energy saving, preferably in the most visible way possible. Unfortunately the most effective solutions are often the least visible, so pursuit of eco-bling can be an expensive mistake. A classic example is the brief popularity of wind turbines a few years ago. They were promoted by politicians mounting them on their homes and also sold off the shelf by a national home-improvement retailer. Although strikingly prominent on a family home, wind turbines are useless in most suburban and urban locations (see below).

The good news is that when you are carrying out building work, incorporating modest but effective sustainable construction principles is not particularly difficult or expensive.

BEWARE OF GREEN STATISTICS

There is now a huge mass of facts and figures available regarding the benefits and costs of making a house more energy efficient. The problem is that they tend to contradict each other. The reason is that it depends on the design and construction of house that is used as a baseline to carry out the analysis. So if you look at the effect of providing extra roof insulation to a very old house that has

A solar collecting roof at the Centre for Alternative Technology in Wales, that turns the sun's rays into electric current.

no insulation in the roof at all to start with, the energy saved as a result is significant. If the same level of roof insulation is added to a house that already has some fitted in accordance with the current regulations, the effect is relatively small by comparison. If a ground-source heat pump is introduced into a well-insulated house, with low-temperature underfloor heating, but the high-temperature water required for hot taps is generated by a separate source, such as an electric water heater, the system will be quite efficient. However, a house that uses normal high-temperature panel radiators, has its hot-water supply on the system and is poorly insulated, will not perform efficiently with a ground-source heat pump and this would be a poor investment. In the latter building, there is a far better return if the money is spent upgrading the insulation. The companies that market energy-efficient products are experts at using the statistics to make their particular bit of kit sound like it will save a small fortune in energy bills, provided that they can pick and choose their statics.

HOW TO BE GREEN

1. Use Less Energy

The simplest way to lower the amount of energy that needs to be supplied to a house to run it, is to use less of it.

Insulation

If a house has poor insulation, increasing it will save a lot of energy and therefore money over the rest of the life of a building. Increasing the insulation to as high a level as is practical is the first energy-efficiency measure that should be carried out. Unless the house is already very well insulated, this is very cost-effective. If the existing walls already have a cavity that is without insulation, it is not expensive to have it filled. Government subsidies are available in the UK to help with the cost.

If the walls are solid either the inside or outside has to be lined with insulation. Dry lining inside the house causes a lot of disruption, so may only be worth doing if a room is to be redecorated and rewired anyway. The depth of the insulation lining means the wall construction is thicker and room sizes will be reduced. External insulation, concealed with render or cladding, is quite costly and may involve altering window sills and other details around the house, but will leave existing rooms untouched. If a new wall is being built for an extension, then, if possible, install at least 150mm of insulation filling into the cavity.

Increasing the depth of the insulation in the loft is easy and cost-effective up to a depth of about 350mm. Other measures to consider are fixing insulation between the floor joists of a timber ground floor and around the hot-water storage cylinder.

Double-Glazing

Replacement double-glazing is only worth considering if the existing windows are single glazed, in poor condition and in need of replacement. Otherwise it is more of a luxury, since it will take decades to pay back the cost in energy savings. If UPVC is used, this requires a lot of energy to be manufactured, also causing pollution. On the plus side, although it is expensive, double-glazing is an

> **Hot Tip**
>
> The single most cost-effective way of making an average UK house construction more energy efficient is to upgrade the existing insulation levels and ensure that new additions are also highly insulated.

improvement on the single-pane variety not just because it has a higher insulation value, but also because modern, well-made windows fit more tightly into the openings and reduce draughts.

Airtight Construction

After increasing the insulation thickness, the second most cost-effective measure for an old house is to reduce the air-flow through it. Once a house is well insulated, the energy-efficiency benefits of adding more layers will not justify the cost. If it is quite draughty, sealing up the gaps around windows, doors and through chimneys will have a big effect, for a relatively small outlay. It is very hard to get an old house completely airtight, but if this is achieved, a ventilation system should be introduced to ensure that sufficient fresh air reaches the occupants.

Low-Energy Fittings

A simple, cheap and often cost-effective way of reducing energy costs is to use electrical products that have a low-energy demand. Low-energy lightbulbs easily cover their extra cost in the energy they save in a few months, when compared to old-fashioned standard lightbulbs. This is why in Europe the latter are no longer to be manufactured. Most electrical appliances, such as washing machines, are coded according to their energy efficiency.

Efficient Boilers and Heating System

If your existing boiler is not a condensing boiler, it makes sense to have it replaced with a modern high-efficiency model. Condensing boilers recover some of the heat that would otherwise be lost in the exhaust gases, by recycling the heat gained into the system. Combi boilers instantaneously

Combining underfloor heating with a ground-source heat-pump requires some sophisticated plumbing.

heat up water as it is needed and are very efficient, provided that there is not a lot a demand and so are ideal for couples, small families or people living on their own. There are government-backed schemes available that will, in some cases, subsidize the replacement of very old boilers.

Ensuring that all the main radiators in the house have thermostatic radiator valves (TRVs) will help to reduce your fuel bills. TRVs allow the room temperatures to be set much lower in some rooms, such as bedrooms, without the need for sophisticated and expensive program controls. When rooms are heated to different temperatures, doors should always be kept closed. Underfloor heating is worth considering, if you are planning major alterations to your house. The heat is more evenly distributed, it is easier to control and more efficient. It also reduces air-currents and draughts.

Daylight
By designing any new rooms to allow maximum daylight, the need for electric lighting can be reduced in the evening. The best daylight levels are gained by windows through which you can see mostly sky. Windows looking on to buildings and landscape are gaining light that is reflected off these surfaces and therefore less effective. Rooflights are excellent sources of natural light for this reason. If the time that you have to switch your lights on in the evening is later, you will be saving energy without even noticing and probably find the rooms more pleasant to use.

Use Biomass Fuels
'Biomass' usually means wood, either in its natural form as logs, or manufactured, wooden pellets. The latter are easier to handle and allow stoking of the fire to be automatic, because it is reconstituted in a standard shape and size. Wood is considered more environment-friendly because wood can be easily regenerated in a few decades in the form of trees, which also in turn extract the carbon back out of the atmosphere. Also, far less carbon is released into the atmosphere when it burns, compared to fossil fuels.

Live a Green Lifestyle

This is a huge topic, not covered by this book, but it is worth considering ideas such as setting the thermostat 1°C lower than you are used to (saving up to 10 per cent of your space heating bills) and switching off appliances rather than keeping them on standby. One of the most effective energy-saving measures that you can make in winter is to ensure you wear a warm jumper when you are in the house, rather than being in your shirtsleeves.

2. Generate Your Own Energy

Most people do not have much option as to how energy is supplied to their house – with a few exceptions, most have a choice of mains electricity, and either mains gas or stored fuel, such as oil, gas or coal. It is usually prohibitively expensive for most people to avoid reliance on external power altogether, but it is possible to use alternative methods to gather some energy from other sources.

Photovoltaic Panels

These are relatively sophisticated panels that are designed to generate electricity, on cloudy days as

Photovoltaic panels generate electricity that can be used or fed back into the National Grid.

well as in direct sunlight. In the UK, large surface areas are necessary to generate significant levels of power and they are expensive relative to the energy that they produce. However, in England and Wales they have been made more economic by the introduction of 'feed-in tariffs'. This scheme pays a subsidy to the homeowner for each unit of electricity created by the solar panels, even if it is used for the house. A higher subsidy is paid for any electricity not used by the homeowner, which is fed into the National Grid. Without a subsidy and a good, south-facing roof to mount them on, photovoltaic panels are effectively a luxury product.

Solar Thermal Collector

One of the simplest and oldest form of energy efficiency device is the solar collector, that consists of pipes filled with water, painted black under a panel of glass. Water or other liquids run through the pipes and heat up. This heat energy is directed to a cylinder and used to 'pre-warm' cold water. In other words, cold water is made lukewarm before it is heated by a boiler. This doesn't sound like much, but it can save a significant amount of energy. The problem is that their peak of efficiency occurs in the middle of the summer, which is when the heat is least needed, so a lot of the potential benefits are wasted. Without a subsidy, such a system could take ten to fifteen years to recover its cost in energy savings. However, the government has made available a renewable heat incentive (RHI) payment to cover some of the installation costs, as well as paying a small amount for each kilowatt of energy generated by this type of solar panel. If you really want to keep costs down, a DIY system of a radiator painted black under a sheet of glass could be more cost-effective than an off-the-shelf product, but you will not get the subsidy unless an approved installer and kit are used.

Passive Solar Gain

When the sun passes through glass, it heats up the surfaces of a room (*see* the explanation of the greenhouse effect in the section on conservatories in Chapter 6). Heat energy passes less easily through glass than light energy and cannot escape as quickly, so it builds up inside as the sun continues to shine. This 'greenhouse' effect can be a benefit, particularly in winter when the location, orientation and design of the windows can provide free heating. In summer, the problem is the reverse – the heat is an unwanted nuisance. By careful design of shading to the windows, the heat from the high summer sun can be excluded, whilst allowing the low-level winter sun to reach the glazed areas.

Ground-Source Heat-Pumps

These systems are effectively a fridge in reverse, in that they extract heat from a liquid, pump the liquid underground, where is it warmed by the natural heat of the subsoil, and then sent back to have this heat extracted again. At their best, they produce approximately three units of energy for every one unit taken to run them. The hotter the water in the heating system has to be, the less efficient the heat pump. They work better with systems that require lower temperatures, such as underfloor heating. If used to heat water to the level required by a hot tap, the heat-exchanger usually needs to be backed up by direct electric heating, hence the drop in efficiency. If mains gas is not available to a house, they are worth considering seriously as an alternative to oil or electricity for space heating.

Wind Turbines

These are a waste of money for houses in urban and suburban areas. This is because the streets and buildings lower the speed of the wind, creating many changes in wind direction and gusts. Wind turbines rely on a strong, consistent wind to be efficient and you are only likely to get this in a rural area or out at sea. With feed-in tariffs to subsidize them, they may be more cost-effective, and certainly larger group schemes in the countryside can pay their way.

3. Recycle

Building Materials

There is a huge range of commercially available recycled building materials, including chipboard, newspaper-based insulation and rubber cladding and floor coverings. A few buildings are built from the material without any processing, such as 'earth-ships', which are made from discarded rubber tyres filled with earth. Sometimes it is possible to re-use bricks and roof tiles. Occasionally, building rubble, generated by the demolition of an existing part of the house, can be crushed and used for hardcore. There is also a thriving trade in architectural salvage, where period features, such as fireplaces, wrought iron gates and even doors, are sold at a premium.

In addition to building with recycled materials, you can also build in such a way that allows the construction to be recycled at the end of its useful life. There are many materials that can be recycled, such as timber for windows, doors, steel used for structural support, slates, tiles and bricks – provided that they have been laid in a soft lime mortar that can easily be cleaned off (modern hard cement mortars stick firmly to bricks, making them difficult to reclaim).

Water Recycling

Surface water, such as the rain that drains off the roof, can easily be collected and re-used for the garden by the traditional water butt. If you want to go to the next level, you can channel all the rainwater into an underground tank and pump it up whenever it is needed, using it to flush toilets as well. 'Grey' water, from sinks, baths and washing machines can also be used to flush toilets, but

Rainwater can be collected in an underground tank and then used for watering the garden, flushing toilets or even drinking water.

requires relatively expensive treatment for any other use. It is possible to treat surface water to the point that it can be drinkable, but again this is usually too elaborate for most homeowners.

4. Use Green Products and Materials

Natural Building Products

Some people believe that the modern, highly manufactured materials incorporated into houses are unhealthy. There is plenty of evidence to show that the paints and plastic products used do give off small quantities of gas, although it has not been proven that they pose a significant health risk, excepting a small group of people who suffer from allergies. Aside from perceived health benefits, natural building materials require less processing and therefore place a greatly reduced demand on energy and resources. It is perfectly possible to build extensions out of straw bales, cob (straw and mud), rubber tyres or rammed earth. All of these have a reduced impact on the environment. Timber, a more mainstream material, locks up carbon and is suitable for building with very little processing beyond cutting it to shape. Preservative treatments can involve some fairly noxious chemicals, but these are not needed if the wood is protected from becoming damp once it is in place.

'Pollution' can be used to describe the contents of your drains and waste bin. It can partly be dealt with by your lifestyle, rather than how the house is built; for example, by separating out rubbish that can be recycled. The pollution caused by waste water can be dealt with in several ways, depending on how keen you are to follow through a green lifestyle.

Local Suppliers

If you are genuinely trying to build sustainably, you should take account of the energy and resources taken to manufacture and transport products and materials to the site. A highly energy-efficient component, such as argon-filled triple-glazing, will undoubtedly reduce the heating cost of the house. However, in terms of the energy cost to the whole planet, the saving, once it is in use, may be completely offset by the huge amount of energy required to make the glass and frames, manufacture the product and then, crucially, ship it from Sweden to your home. This problem is insurmountable in practical terms for most homeowners, although some may be fortunate enough to have local suppliers of some building products, such as claypits used for bricks.

Green Roofs

These are increasingly being used in urban areas, where they help to promote biodiversity, i.e. encourage butterflies and other creatures. Some use grass, but it will need a lot of looking after, so a succulent plant called sedum, which requires less maintenance, is very popular. These roofs need a strong structure to support them, as well as an effective waterproof membrane underneath to prevent leaks. This means that they are more expensive compared to a normal flat roof and have a much thicker construction. If the planners will not allow a flat roof because they don't like the appearance, a green roof may be acceptable to them as an alternative.

Green roofs are expensive, but also are a very environment-friendly feature, especially in built-up areas.

How Much Does it Cost?

The following are for a typical 1950s three-bedroom house, 2010 prices.

Increase insulation levels in roof: £200–£400. Sheep's wool and recycled plastic can be used, as well as the more traditional mineral wool insulation.
Add cavity wall insulation: £300–£600. Houses built after 1928 are likely to have a cavity, allowing up to 40 per cent reduction in heat loss by filling them with mineral wool or polystyrene.
Draughtproofing: £80–£150. Very effective and can be a DIY job.
Energy-efficient lighting: £30–£50. Very quick payback and easily done.
More efficient boiler: £1,500–£2,000. Important step if the existing boiler is old and is not a condensing boiler.
Solar hot-water system: £3,500–£4,000. Can provide up to a third of your water-heating demand. Payback very long without subsidy, and roof has to have right orientation.
Biomass boiler: £7,000–£9,000. Boiler and fuel storage will need more space than a compact gas boiler.
Double-glazing: £6,000–£10,000. Only worth doing if the existing single glazing is in poor condition.
Photovoltaics: £5,000–£10,000. As with a hot-water system, orientation is important. Poor payback, compensated by feed-in tariffs in the UK.
Wind turbine: £3,000–£5,000. Pointless unless you are in a very exposed location, e.g. on a high hill or on the coast.

The problem for anyone who wishes to make environmentally friendly alterations to their house is that it may take decades for the savings in running costs to cover the cost of the work. It is a lifestyle choice, rather than a financial one, and it is unwise to spend too much on it unless you expect to live in the house for many years into the future. However, environmental assessments of buildings are enshrined in many of the current building regulations in the UK. Like new properties, existing houses have to be energy rated and given a 'green label' to indicate the level of energy efficiency represented by the finished construction when they are sold. Future purchasers of your home will have information available to enable an assessment to be made of the costs of heating and lighting, and whether or not it is an environmentally friendly home. As energy costs rise, houses that score as highly efficient will sell for a higher price than those that do not, making any environmentally friendly improvements that have been incorporated cost-effective.

Feed-In Tariffs

These government initiatives work by paying householders a subsidy for generating energy on-site. They were necessary because otherwise the small scale makes it hard to justify the costs. For example, under a scheme introduced by the UK government in 2009, the first householders who installed photovoltaic panels on their house were paid 41.3p for every KWh generated for their own use, although this amount reduces over time. Financial experts say that this is the equivalent of 8 per cent return on the money invested. Any excess electricity is fed into the grid and attracts a slightly higher subsidy.

Similar schemes are available for ground-source heat-pumps, solar panels and wind turbines, known as the Renewable Heat Incentive (RHI).

The downside is that it is paid for by increasing the electricity bills of everyone who does not enter the scheme, as an incentive for people to join it.

Planning the Construction Stage

Once you have planning and building regulations approval, you may be tempted to think that no more design work is needed and that you are ready to get some prices from contractors. But the level of information that the local authority officers require is not sufficient to describe all the building work that will be necessary for a contractor to price or build from. The building control officer is not concerned about the decorations or choice of taps, but details of the fittings, decorations and the like have to be specified by someone, ideally before building work starts on site.

How and when that detail is worked out, and who decides it all depends on how you intend to run the project. There are four main options. Which you pick will depend not only on your own skills and budget but also how much time you can devote to the project to become involved in its day-to-day running.

MAIN CONTRACTOR: DESIGN AND BUILD

This option is best if you want only minimal involvement in the detailed design and construction, and can afford the luxury of significant extra cost. You can engage the contractor at a very early stage, usually before planning (although it can be later). If you ask for a fixed price from several contractors before the building has been fully designed, it is impossible to compare them and identify who is offering best value for money. In order to quote a price, they will have to make a lot of assumptions. A decent builder will assume a good-quality construction, whereas one who is less conscientious will base his price on rock-bottom quality and then charge for all sorts of extras once the project is on site. If you go to just one contractor for a price, there is no competition and so you will not necessarily get a keen price. If the contractor takes responsibility for preparing and submitting the drawings, they retain the copyright for the design and you will be obliged to use them to build the project, or pay a large fee to use them with someone else. Even if the drawing work is described as 'thrown in for free', you will in fact be paying for it. It puts you in a much better bargaining position if you pay the designer that money directly and they can give you independent advice.

MAIN CONTRACTOR: BUILD-ONLY

Most people will choose to employ a builder to

Good, professional builders have great skill and are worth paying to get the job done properly.

do all the building work. Apart from getting a good price, you need to find a company that will proceed quickly and who can anticipate and solve the inevitable problems that develop in the course of the building work. Speed is important because the disruption caused to the everyday lives of a family is considerable, even for a loft conversion where a lot of the work goes on above the living areas. To get the full benefit you must agree a fixed price before you agree to employ the builder. This way the risk of extras and unexpected problems lies mainly with them and, although extra costs are almost inevitable in any building project, they should not be excessive.

You engage an architect to prepare your own detailed specifications and drawings, and invite fixed-price tenders from several builders. Once appointed, the builder is responsible for ensuring that the building is completed on time and budget, to the specified level of quality. You also have the option of employing an architect to deal with the day-to-day management, approve payments, ensure the specification is followed and to keep an eye on quality.

SELF-MANAGE

If you want more involvement on site but don't have the time or inclination to actually do the build-

ing work, you can hire individual trades, either on a fixed price or daily rate, to do it for you. You then will take on the role that is usually played by the main contractor, i.e. buying some of the materials, find and employing individuals and subcontractors, performing the site-management role, and possibly doing some of the less critical work (e.g. decorating). Money is saved because you do not have to pay as much for overheads as a contractor, and you keep all of the profit they would otherwise take out of the project. If you use small companies who are below the VAT threshold, you can achieve a further reduction in cost. Builders' merchants' discounts and so on that cannot be achieved by domestic customers, may reduce savings in the same way as for someone carrying out a DIY project.

However, it is a mistake to think that builders earn their profit easily. It is usually hard-won by bargaining, shrewd business acumen and the skilful management of people. As a self-manager you will have to go some way to matching these skills in order to make the exercise worthwhile. As well as management skills, you also need time to apply them – not just a certain number of hours in the week, but you sometimes have to be available at specific points of the day as well. If a problem develops, it may have to be sorted out straight away, and deliveries of supplies may require you to be there to check and sign for them. For this reason, many self-managers tend to be people whose job allows them flexible working hours, such as the self-employed or senior management. A common problem for self-managers is that subcontractors and trades fail to turn up on the appointed day, or leave a job part-way through. This is because they can afford to offend (and lose) a one-off client, and will risk that rather than let down a contractor who employs them regularly, who needs them at short notice.

Apart from assuming the role of the contractor, you also assume most of the risks. A builder who quotes a fixed price gambles on his ability to price accurately and properly manage the project. If they do well, they make more profit. If they do badly, they will lose money, but the cost to the client is the same. If you are managing the project and it goes wrong, you will lose money or, in the worst case, run out of funding and have to stop the whole project. Conversely, the rewards are potentially high if you are successful at it.

To take this route successfully it is sensible to have the design and specification worked out well before each stage or trade is started, so that payment can be agreed and the work programmed in. However, you will be able to incorporate products and materials that you discover as the project proceeds on site. You can also trim or expand the amount you spend on fittings and finishes more easily towards the end of the building work.

DIY

Taking on most of the building work yourself is an option that should only be taken up by the most determined of home-improvement enthusiasts. It is possible, but rare, for anyone to actually complete every task personally – not least because some work should definitely be carried out by people with training and qualifications, such as electrical wiring or fitting boilers. The main lure for working this way, apart from the challenge, is the reduction in cost achieved by cutting out the profit taken by the main contractor and the expense of hiring labour. The benefits have increased in recent times, due to the lack of skilled building workers and the consequent increase in their wages. However,

these savings can be partially offset by the builders' merchants and suppliers charging higher prices. They are reluctant to offer DIY enthusiast the same level of discount available to long-term customers.

Apart from the reduced costs, the other common feature of the DIY route is the extra time required to complete the project. It can take two or three times longer than an experienced contractor. The pressure to complete means that most leisure time is taken up working on the site. Progress is slowed, as new skills have to be learnt and old ones are brushed up. Apart from the building work, all the management side has to be dealt with as well. Health and safety, insurance, ordering of materials and dealing with building control officers, all need to be accounted for. Sometimes, to avoid these kind of difficulties, a hybrid of the full DIY route is used when the large-scale construction work is built by a professional contractor, leaving a watertight shell for the self-builders to then arrange the electrical installation, plumbing, plastering and decorating themselves.

Although you should have a carefully monitored cost plan, and you must comply with planning and building regulations, you are free to make design decisions and change the specification as work progresses. Any design decisions taken from an early stage must allow for ease of construction and products or construction methods that require a high level of building skill not possessed by the DIY enthusiast are best avoided. For example, structural alterations should be kept simple, and new roof shapes should be kept straightforward (possibly avoiding hips in favour of gables).

TENDERS AND COST CONTROL

When the building is ready to start on site, good cost-control is achieved by ensuring that the builder has quoted a fixed figure, enshrined in a sound, well-written contract. The unpleasant surprise of excessive extra costs arising as work proceeds can be avoided by having a clear agreement on price at the start. Once a building company is on site, you usually have to use them for any extra work so it is harder to negotiate. If you have had an architect prepare a thoroughly detailed set of plans

How choice of building method affects a project			
	Main Contractor: Design and Build	**Main Contractor: Build-Only**	**Self-Manage**	**DIY**
---	---	---	---	---
Price	Fixed at planning	Fixed at tender	Updated as building proceeds	Updated as building proceeds
Quality	Completely under contractor's control	Strictly controlled by you, often through an architect	Controlled by project manager or you day to day	Controlled by you day to day
Copyright	Rests with the contractor – you have to use them if you want to build their design	Rests with whoever prepared the the drawings, but you own the right to use the design for your project	Rests with whoever prepared the drawings, but you own the right to use the design for your project	Rests with whoever prepared the drawings, but you own the right to use the design for your project
Risk and responsibility for problems	Mostly with contractor	Split between you, the architect and the contractor	Mostly you, with some with tradesmen	All with you
Management time invested by you	Minimal	Average, but depends on how much you delegate to the architect	Lots of time needed, often during the working week	Very high time-commitment
Amount of drawings and specification required	Drawings by builder, outline specifications only, no detailed drawings	Full working drawings and specifications, all worked out before tenders invited	Either building regulations drawings only, or tender package prepared by architect	Usually building regulations drawings only produced by an architect
Site management	Contractor	Contractor or architect	You, or your project manager	You
Choice of materials	Mostly chosen by contractor	Mostly chosen by you, sometimes with an architect advising	You, helped by each contractor	You
Insurances	Contractor	Contractor	You	You
Responsibility for health and safety	Contractor	Contractor	You or your project manager	You
Payment	At agreed stages	At agreed stages	At stages or end of each week	As needed, or with an account at a builders' merchant
Detailed programme	Controlled by contractor	Controlled by contractor, sometimes monitored by an architect	Controlled by you or your project manager	Controlled by you and your family

and specifications, you can hold the builder to the quote agreed in the contract, and if there are any genuine extras, they are easy to identify. Provided that you have taken the precaution of getting a price breakdown of each element of the job before the builder was appointed, it will be relatively easy to work out a fair price for extras.

Apart from good documentation, take a methodical approach to finding the right builder. Prepare a long list, whittling it down to your favoured few and then, after you have received tenders and picked the most likely candidates, make more in-depth checks to ensure that your final decision is sound. In the current economic climate, a credit check is advisable if you do not know the company.

For any project, however small, obtain an absolute minimum of three quotes, if possible. For larger domestic projects, get at least four or five. Because builders are constantly tendering for projects they may initially indicate a willingness to tender, then drop out before the submission date because they have been successful with another project. Always add one two more than your minimum requirement to be sure of getting enough prices to be confident that you will get a good range. Bear in mind that you are likely to be dealing with small businesses with limited manpower. The boss will spend most of the day managing sites and leave the preparation of tenders to the evenings and weekends. They will want to subcontract to plumbers, plasterers and electricians, who in turn will have to prepare their own figures to feed into the final price tendered. All this takes time, so to get a reliable figure, allow an adequate tender period. For a small project this should be no less than three weeks, preferably four. For a more complex project, four or five weeks is reasonable. Whilst the builders are preparing their prices, they should visit the site or the existing building. If they ask a lot of questions, this is probably a good thing, because it shows that they are reading the information that they have been given and considered it carefully. However, if you give any extra details to one, it is essential to pass this on to all the others. If you don't, you will not be able to compare 'like with like' when the prices come back.

Finally, once you have chosen your builder, work should not start until the written contract has been signed. Do not use the builder's standard contract, or one prepared by the contractors' organizations – these are usually heavily biased against your interests. If any terms are written in faint grey text on the back of the quote, you should cross them out and exclude them in writing from any agreement. The reason they are so hard to read is because the builder is hoping you won't bother to look at them too closely. Fortunately there are some standard contracts easily available from most bookshops, prepared by the Joint Contracts Tribunal (JCT), that have been agreed by all sectors of the construction industry as fair and reasonable. The contract terms include provisions that make unfair increases in cost by the contractor very difficult.

BUILDING CONTRACTORS

Whether you are looking for a company to do the whole job, or someone to do the plumbing, there are some basic rules to follow in selecting a builder that apply across the board. Obviously the less significant the role, the less intensive the selection procedure, and it is up to you to decide how many of the suggestions that are listed here are taken up.

You should aim to get at least three or four prices. But you should probably contact more than this initially. This is because whether or not a building contractor from a smaller company will submit a price is influenced by their workload, which can change overnight when they win a contract. It is not unusual for a contractor to agree to tender one day, and have a change of mind the next. They may let you know they have changed their mind, but are more likely to not bother to submit a price. Alternatively, they may inflate their tender to an unrealistically high figure, so that if by some accident they do get the job, it will have a very big profit margin to compensate for the need to employ extra staff. A reasonable number of contractors to approach with a preliminary enquiry is five or possibly six, allowing for one or two to drop out, or overprice. The minimum to aim for is three tendered prices.

Building work is not licensed, which means that anyone can be a builder and advertise themselves as such. The first step to finding a good, genuinely skilled builder is to make up a list of likely firms and whittle it down by investigating each firm. Contractors who are good at what they do, don't have to advertise – they get much of their work through happy clients recommending them to their friends.

Check for recommendations from:

- Your architect.
- Yellow Pages.
- Local papers.
- Friends.
- Neighbours.
- Builders' merchants and product suppliers.
- Site boards by building sites.
- Internet sites that list contractors and have feedback from previous customers.
- Pro-active contractors who contacted you after your planning application was submitted.
- Local authority planners and building control officers (strictly unofficially).
- Local authority lists of approved contractors, which are sometimes available to the public.

It is crucial to the success of your project that you engage the right building contractor, so you must carry out a thorough selection procedure. None of the ways that you can obtain names are particularly reliable in themselves, but you will then have a shortlist to work on. Basic checks are followed by more detailed scrutiny of those who seem most promising.

Checking Out Building Contractors – First Stage

The suggestions for investigations you can carry out listed below apply to general builders. Individuals who carry out minor maintenance or have a single trade work in a different way.

Can You Easily Get a Full Name and Address?
If there is just a mobile phone number and no evidence of a proper address on their business card or letterhead, treat them with caution. If there are details, do they give their home telephone number? Do they have a yard or an office, or have you been given just an accommodation address? A small business may be able to keep their prices down by avoiding overheads, but if your project is significant you will need a well-organized, well-resourced contractor.

Membership of Organizations
There are plenty of organizations for builders. Some require members to satisfy a very simple requirement in order to join. Others require nothing more than a membership fee. Some are glorified marketing organizations, with the main aim being to represent and procure work for their members. The truly professional organizations that builders may belong to are the RICS (Royal Institute of Chartered Surveyors), the NFB (National Federation of Builders) and the CIOB (Chartered Institute of Building). These organizations require proper qualifications and enforce codes of conduct. All the other builders' organizations, whatever grand claims they make, are effectively clubs or lobby groups for the benefit of their members. Once they have your details, a few will even try to sell you insurance policies or finance. Membership of this type of organization is not a guarantee of a good-quality service.

Just because they have a logo on their van, it does not mean that they are genuinely members of the organization. Dodgy contractors regularly misrepresent their membership because it gives false reassurance to their victims. If you are in any doubt, it is very easy to check with these bodies to verify any such claims.

Track Record
How long has the company been trading? This is not the same as how long they have been in business. It is possible to wind up a business and start a new company with a very similar name the next day, and employing the same staff at the same premises, avoiding all the debts and legal liabilities of the old company. However, bear in mind that the construction industry is notorious for 'boom and bust' and occasionally, small building firms are made insolvent through no fault of their own; for example, by the poor payment practices by larger companies.

Staff

How many staff do they employ directly, as opposed to contract workers and subcontractors? If there is only one person managing the business, what happens when he goes on holiday or is sick?

Availability

When times are good, the best building contractors tend to be booked up months or even years ahead. Some have their whole year's work set up by the Spring. So if they are available at short notice, ask why. There may be a sound reason; for example, because another contract has fallen through leaving them suddenly without work.

Behaviour and Communication

If whoever you are dealing with doesn't listen to you properly, speaks in jargon or is apparently unwilling to answer straight questions clearly, put a big question mark next to their company, and ask to talk to someone else if they are not in a senior position.

Readiness to Quote

Insist that you require them to quote a fixed price and to use a standard contract. If they prefer to use their own terms and conditions, ask to see a copy. A builder's own contracts and those prepared by some of the 'builders' clubs' are usually heavily biased in their favour. If they suggest that you don't need a written contract, bear in mind that all reputable contractors will insist that one be signed.

Is There a Brochure or Leaflet That Can Be Sent?

Do not be too disappointed if they cannot send you a posh brochure or leaflet in the post. Many excellent builders are not especially good at marketing, because as long as they have happy clients who recommend them, there is always work waiting for them.

Checking Out Building Contractors – Second Stage: Research and Visiting

By this stage you should have whittled your short-list down to the most promising candidates and you can concentrate your more thorough investigations on these remaining few.

Don't put any of them on your tender list unless you feel it is very likely that you would choose them if their price is the most favourable. You may not do all the second-stage checks below until after you have prices back, but it is very important to take the time to complete them before the contract is signed.

Company Office and Yard

Find an excuse to visit their workplace. It is unlikely to be a palace, but it will give you a good impression of the type of firm you are dealing with. An unkempt, scruffy yard will be an indication of what your home will be like if they are working there. The office may be based at home, and the value of the house and make of car in the drive will tell you a bit about the profitability of the company.

References and Portfolio

Most builders are delighted to be given the opportunity to show you examples of previous projects they have completed. Don't just look on the website. Unfortunately it is easy to 'cut and paste' illustrations from rival websites and occasionally this happens. Talk to the builders about how the projects were run and also speak to previous clients when the contractor is not present. If possible, visit some of the buildings to see them in their entirety.

Insurance

All building contractors must have public liability insurance and the other insurance necessary to run a construction site. Ask the contractor to confirm the extent of the cover. They should produce documentary proof for your own records before you sign the contract.

Integrity

There are many ways to evade taxes and save money by ignoring legislation and it is sometimes difficult to resist an offer to reduce the cost in this way, perhaps saving thousand of pounds. If a builder will evade the payment of taxes so unashamedly, they may be just as ready to cheat you in due course. If anything does go wrong, it will be much harder to get redress from a company that operates as part of the 'black economy'.

Many of the tragic stories involving people who have been swindled by builders actually start with a price being offered that is significantly lower than all the others submitted. However tempting it is to go along with this, remember that the old adage 'you never get something for nothing' fits the building trade better than any other area of commerce.

Contrary to the image of the small building contractor promoted by some elements of the press and television, there are many excellent builders in the UK, who take great personal pride in their work and are scrupulously honest in their dealings with their customers. They leave nothing but well-constructed projects and a lot of good will in their wake. If you take the trouble to locate one of these firms, you will find the experience educational and enjoyable. We should all treat such professionals decently and pay them fairly, or they will become an endangered species.

Checking Out Building Contractors – Final Stage: After Tenders

Once you have tenders back and you have one or two preferred contractors, there are still some further checks to make before you can move on to arranging for the contract to be signed.

Check Their Calculations

Ask for a detailed breakdown that lists how they have built up their price. This is a reasonable request and usual in the construction industry, so there is no good reason for them to refuse. Once you have this, check their basic arithmetic to make sure that no obvious mistakes have been made. The process that the builder has to go through to prepare this information for you will require him to double check everything as well.

Check That They Have Been Through All the Tender Documents

Whilst a contractor is preparing a price for a tender, it is usual for them to have questions about aspects of the work, or for there to be some aspect

---

How to Spot a Cowboy

- Reluctance to supply a proper postal address.
- No landline telephone number.
- Logos used when not a member of the organization.
- History of regularly winding up companies.
- Available immediately with no good explanation.
- Lack of politeness and respect from staff.
- Attempt to get you to sign an unreasonable contract.
- Reluctance to work with your professional team.
- Lack of previous clients' contact details for you to follow up.
- Will not produce insurance certificates.
- Attempts made to evade tax, offers 'cash in hand' deals.
- Quotation that is significantly lower than everyone else.
- Demands payment in advance.
- Frequent changes of address.

---

that requires clarification. Occasionally there is an error or ambiguity that may affect the price. If a contractor has been in touch during the tender period asking questions and commenting on the documents, this is a very good sign. It means that they have been thinking carefully about the project and reading everything that they have been sent before submitting a price. It is also normal for them to want to visit the house to gain an impression of the existing building. If there has been no such contact from the tenderer, they should be asked why not. They may have a reasonable explanation or they may have just not properly considered the implications of the project. You may feel that, if the latter has happened, it is better to keep quiet and get a bargain price. This will cause problems for the builder but it is not in your own interests either. One of the main reasons for a serious breakdown between builder and client on site is when the builder has underpriced and started to run out of time and money.

Company Search

If the firm is a limited company, it is relatively cheap and easy to go on to the Companies House website and check their last set of submitted accounts (www.companieshouse.gov.uk). If the builder is a sole trader, this will not show up, and you would have to go to a credit reference agency, such as Experian (www.experian.co.uk) for any information.

Self-Managing Tradesmen or Subcontractors

If you wish to organize you own project and even do some of the building work yourself, the trades that you will employ to help you need to be handled in a different way to a building company. The general principles suggested above still apply, but there are some important differences. These tradesmen are often just individuals and are more difficult to find. They have to give priority to their regular employers – the contractors who use them as part of a building team. They may not wish to agree to a written contract, and any record of your agreement will probably have to be kept by you. They will expect to be paid weekly, not in stages as with a main contractor, and they will probably want cash in hand.

The best way to find them is through recommendation, but sometimes the only way to find out if they are any good is to employ them, monitor them and sack them if they do not perform. It is hard to find good, reliable workers, because even the established contractors have trouble getting them and fewer and fewer younger people are moving into the construction industry to replace the skilled older generation.

Asking for Tenders

The difference between managing the tender process well and managing it badly can be measured in

---

Checklist for Obtaining Quotes Before the Design Has Been Prepared for a Typical Extension

The following is a list of aspects of the work that affect the price. If one builder has included something that another has not, the prices should be adjusted accordingly before comparing them:

- Accommodation – how many bedrooms, bathrooms, etc. and their approximate size.
- Staircase location assumed.
- Number, type, material and approximate size of windows, e.g. two dormers with 1,200 × 1,200mm double-glazed UPVC windows, four 600 × 950mm roof windows.
- Dormer cladding type, e.g. leadwork to gable, tiled sides, double pitched roof.
- Materials to be used and how well they will match the existing house.
- Are there any necessary works to complete the job not included, e.g. tiling, finishes, sanitary ware?
- What works are included for the existing house, e.g. upgrade to the boiler, rewire, new fire doors to bedrooms?
- Detailed specifications of doors, stairs, ironmongery, sanitary fittings, light-switches, paint finishes.
- Level of insulation – will it be the minimum level possible under the regulations or more generous?
- Who obtains and pays for planning and building regulations approval?
- Are the designer's and engineer's fees included?
- Who is responsible for expenses and what are they likely to be?
- Will the builder provide welfare facilities for the workforce, such as a portaloo, and space for preparing drinks, or will they be trooping into the house?
- What security measures will be taken for when the house is unoccupied?
- Types and levels of insurance.
- What are the payments terms? Will money be asked for 'up front', at the end or in stages?

thousands of pounds for a typical project. If you are asking for prices from design build contractors without a tender package, as a very minimum you should ask them to include a detailed specification with their price and also ask them to make it clear whether the figure is an estimate that can be altered later on, or a fixed quotation that will not change as the detail of the project is developed. As mentioned earlier, if a fixed price is quoted, a sensible builder will either want the flexibility to vary the specifications or the price in the event of unexpected work becoming apparent later in the project as the detail is worked out. This will be less of a problem where the likely plan and design is fairly apparent right at the beginning or the house type is a standard one for the area.

If you have your own design and construction drawings prepared, you or your architect will send out tenders to the selected builders requesting a fixed price. A period of three or four weeks is usually allowed for this, as many contractors tend to deal with pricing in between all their site-related jobs for the day, and also they will in turn want to put some of the work out to tender from their regular subcontractors.

When inviting builders to prepare a price, it is essential that they all base their calculations on exactly the same information. Any extra details or changes of mind discussed individually must then be confirmed to all of them. This is the only way that the prices received can be accurately compared. It is also important that they are not told which other builders are on the list. The reason for this

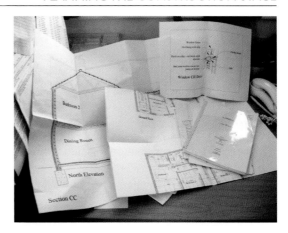

If you want to control cost, a detailed tender package is essential. Author.

is that if they know their competitors' pricing policies, it is possible for them to adjust their tender price accordingly, or in very rare cases fix the price.

Apart from the price, the tender should also state how long the builder will take to complete the work, and when they can start.

BUDGET CHECK

As ever, you should keep an eye on your budget. You should allow a contingency on top of your budget for unexpected items that may crop up on site, or last minute additions that you may wish to make. If you are using a main contractor, this should be a minimum of 10 per cent of the tender price at the start of the construction stage. Some people suggest that you should state a contingency sum in the tender documents. This often happens with commercial projects, where budgets are fixed by managers and need to be included for accounting reasons. There is no need to tell the contractors you have allowed contingencies – in fact if you can convince them that you are breaking the bank to pay for additional items and even a little extra cost will be painful, it might help persuade them to keep their extras at a realistic level.

For a similar reason, you should try to avoid giving the contractor the opportunity to include

---

A Typical Tender Package

A typical tender package will contain:

- Letter inviting tenders.
- Form to reply to tenders.
- Tender return envelope.
- Set of 1:50 plans and elevations.
- Possibly a 1:20 section.
- Possibly some 1:5 details of special features.
- Detailed specification (e.g. ten A4 pages).

Some Typical Items to be Included in a Detailed Specification

If the items listed are not described in your builder's quotation or tender documents, it is essential to ask for them to be specified before signing on the dotted line, particularly if they involve aspects of the work that are important to you.

General Contract Conditions – See later section on contracts for these items.

Excavations – Can any waste spoil be disposed of on site? Topsoil to be retained and re-used on site?

Floors – Precast concrete or standard timber, or timber I-joists Will they be boarded in chipboard or tongue and groove softwood? Is underfloor heating required?

Internal walls – Will they be timber or metal studwork? If studwork, will they be filled with sound-reducing insulation? Will any of the internal walls be fire resistant?

External walls – Masonry or timber frame? Clad in brick, render tile or timber boards? High level of insulation required or the minimum required by building regulations? Any specialist brickwork, e.g. type of sills and heads, dentil courses?

Pitched roof – Clay tiles, interlocking concrete tiles or slate? Tile colour and type, e.g. plain or inter-locking? How will the roof structure be adapted? Will any new roof tiles closely match the existing roof covering? High level of insulation or minimum required by building regulations? Valleys formed from lead or plastic? Will any service penetrations through the roof be concealed with special tiles or just pass through and be visible? How will the roof be accessed? Will proper scaffold be erected or will the roofers try to access the roof just from ladders? The latter may be against health and safety rules.

Flat roof – Standard construction or specialist, such as single ply, zinc or lead? How will the roof be protected from the sun, e.g. white chippings or reflective paint?

Internal doors – Construction, e.g. flush, pressed fibreboard, natural timber, mortice, tenon and wedged? Finish, e.g. self-finished, painted, stained or varnished? Ironmongery type, e.g. brushed aluminium, brass finish, plastic? Ironmongery type, e.g. lever handles, knobs, etc.? Locks, e.g. mortice locks, bolts, etc.?

External doors and windows – Construction, e.g. UPVC, softwood, hardwood? Glazing, e.g. safety glass, triple glazing, argon units? Style, e.g. plain casements, cottage style, Georgian, real or fake leaded lights? Ironmongery finish and type?

---

in their tender what are known as 'prime cost sums' and 'provisional sums'. Both of these are used by a contractor to avoid fixing the price. They are suggested costs for some items of the work that can be revised as work progresses (usually upwards). If the work can be fully described and the contractor is competent, it should be possible to quote a fixed price.

What to Do If You Go Over Budget

Even if you have planned your project carefully, there is still a risk of going over budget when you receive tenders. This is because the prices for small contract works are inherently difficult to predict. If the tender prices are very much higher, this may mean you have to abandon the project; but assum-

ing you have had good advice and followed it, it is more likely that you will have to carry out a cost reduction exercise.

Now you have a real figure to work on plus a builder who can suggest savings and give you the actual savings that are possible for any changes that you may consider. You need to identify the reasons for going over budget and take action accordingly.

The following are some of the reasons that a project cost comes in too high at tender stage.

High Specification

It is human nature to want better quality fixtures, fittings and finishes than are affordable – a major cause of going over budget. If this is the problem, at least it is relatively easy to put right, by going

Joinery – Staircase construction e.g. natural timber or MDF and plywood? Staircase joinery style, e.g. handrails, banisters and newel posts, open or cut strings? Who fits the kitchen, and do they do other things, e.g, lighting and tiling? Fitted cupboards and airing cupboard construction and appearance? Skirtings, trims and architraves – style, profile and material, e.g. MDF or softwood?

Sanitary goods – Manufacturer and model number? Taps, e.g. chrome, brass finish, monoblock, thermostatic mixer? WC suite lid type? Vanity units?

Heating system – Will the existing system be thoroughly checked? Can the existing boiler cope with the extra demand of new rooms to heat? Boiler type, e.g. combination, mains pressured, condensing? Will the boiler system have rust inhibitor added when refilled after the work is completed? Heating method underfloor, radiators, air blown, perimeter heating (in a kitchen)? Will all work to the heating system or gas supply pipes be carried out by a qualified plumber? (Note this is actually required by law. The approved body that regulates a plumber's work used to be called CORGI. This name is quite well known but it no longer applies. The correct regulating body since 1 April 2009 has been Capita Gas Registration and Ancillary Services Limited.)

Electrical services – Numbers of all sockets, lights and switches for each room, located on a plan if possible. Types of fitting, e.g. security lights wall mounted, pendants, bulkhead fittings? Special circuits, e.g. electric cooker? Other wiring, e.g. computer networking cable, TV sockets, security system? (Note: work must be carried out by a qualified electrician. Test certificate to be issued on completion. As with gas installations, the Electrical Contractors Association, which used to be the body that governed the certification process, has been replaced since April 2009 by a subsidiary company of that organization called EC Certification Limited. This is the name that any certification should be issued under.)

Surface finishes – Is decoration of all surfaces inside and out included? Will all making good of existing surfaces damaged by the work be included? Walls – papered or painted? Ceiling – any textured finishes? Floor, e.g. quarry tiles, laminated, carpeted? Wall tiling, where and to what extent?

External works – Will any areas of the garden and land surrounding the house be made good if they are affected by the works? Any new work required? If so, detailed specifications should be agreed, e.g. there is a big difference between a cheap tarmac covering and a properly laid tarmac drive. Location of areas available to the contractor for storage.

through everything with the builder and getting an idea on where money can be saved on individual items.

Tender Process Has Gone Wrong
If you have only received one or two tenders when you have sent out four or five, there will be a reason that the others have not bothered. They may be the wrong sort of builders for your project, or they may just be very busy. A poorly presented or confusing set of tender documents often results in higher tenders being submitted, because the contractors put in extra costs to cover the uncertainty. If they don't do this, they will rely on adding lots of extras on site to compensate. If the prices that you have received are too high, it may be worth re-tendering to a fresh set of builders.

Making a Bad Impression
Sometimes builders will drop out of the tender process or inflate their price as a direct result of meeting their potential customer. Professional advisors are reluctant to admit it, but there is no doubt that sometimes it is better for the homeowner not to say too much to the builders when tenders are being prepared. If you come across as unreasonably picky or demanding, or as having unrealistically high expectations, or you give them the impression that you will require lots of long meetings to discuss the minutiae of every aspect of the project, this will result in high tenders from builders. If you want a good standard of work it is important that this is made clear, but you must be careful how you put this across when meeting prospective contractors.

Corruption

Very occasionally some of the builders in a local area get together and exchange information about the jobs they are pricing. They then agree who will get the job and everyone submits artificially high prices. This is illegal and rare in the area of the construction industry that deals with house alterations. Most examples that have been uncovered involve large commercial or public contracts. One way of safeguarding against this is to send out to a broad mix of companies, and to include at least one who is not in the immediate neighbourhood.

The Economy

Over the time it takes to get a project designed, approved and out to tender, prices may fluctuate. If the market is moving up quickly and there is a lot of work available, prices can go up relatively quickly. Most home alterations attract VAT and the government of the day may put this up, adding to your anticipated cost. It may be possible to take some elements out of the contract and pay tradesmen directly who are not VAT registered, e.g. decorators. Alternatively, re-tendering at a less busy time of the year may help to keep the price down. For example, builders are keener to tender for work in the period of winter before Christmas.

The Scheme is Too Big for Your Budget

If you can't actually afford the scheme that you would like, ideally you should know this before you send it out for tender. However, if tenders are so high that the suggestions in the box will not make enough difference, it is worth considering a re-design before you abandon the project altogether. If the scheme is more modest, it should be relatively easy to get through the planning process and to save time, the amendment of the detailed drawings could proceed whilst you are awaiting approval. If you also manage to keep the contractor on board, the delay and extra cost of reworking the scheme may not be prohibitive.

How to Reduce the Cost

Decorations and finishes – Choose more simple finishes with a narrower range of colours. Do your own decorating. Take out any special finishes, use plain white finishes. Omit finishes that can be changed later, such as laminate floors and quarry tiles, and replace them with budget vinyls and carpets, to be upgraded later.

Internal doors and ironmongery – Internal doors can be replaced easily, so to start with fit the cheapest you can bear, and replace them one by one as you can afford it. Fit cheaper doors to rooms that are not on show, such as first-floor bedrooms.

Kitchens – Many fitted kitchens from specialist suppliers are greatly overpriced compared to a general contractor fitting them, but ensure that a skilled joiner is doing the work. A very cheap kitchen may not look the part, but again can be replaced once your finances have recovered.

Joinery, skirtings and trims – Swap decorative or fancy skirting and architraves with simple plain profiles. Use softwood instead of hardwood, or, if it is painted and indoors, with MDF. Buy cheap furniture units rather than pay the contractor to install fitted furniture.

Electrical installations – It is quite common for lighting schemes to be overdesigned and specified by home improvers. Use cheaper light fittings that can be replaced later as long as the concealed wiring is in the right position.

Sanitary ware – Plain, white, low-cost fittings may not look as good but are usually as comfortable to use as the more expensive ones.

Special features – If you selected underfloor heating, central vacuum cleaning, solar panels or expensive fire surrounds, re-assess how badly you want them.

Garage – Some whole elements of the building can be omitted without destroying the scheme. Detached garages can be built later or substituted with a cheaper one made from precast concrete panels (if planning approval is not an obstacle).

External works – External work can be quite expensive, especially if large areas are involved. A cheap gravel drive can be used as a base for brick pavers to be laid later.

Managing a Building Project

Once you have obtained the necessary local authority approvals and found the right builder for you project, you will be almost ready for building work to start. But there are still one or two issues that need to be addressed first. You should have a proper written contract that clarifies the services that the builder is going to provide for you. There is some preparation work that you can do to ensure that you can deal with the demands and disruption that will be inflicted on you as a result of major construction work being carried out on the house where you and your family are living.

The success or failure of the construction stage will probably have been decided well before you

Probably the most exciting point in the whole process is when the builders arrive on site and start digging the foundations.

reach this point. Things will go wrong, because that's what happens on a building site, even the most thorough planning cannot cover every eventuality. But if you accept that there will be problems, and have an idea of how they will be dealt with, you have every chance of dealing with them successfully. Much of this section applies if you are using a builder to do all the organization and work for you. It is possible to delegate a lot of the responsibility for some of the tasks, provided that this is clearly stated in the contract. If you are self-managing separate trades or doing much of the work yourself, it is essential that you fully understand what is needed to help the project to run smoothly.

If the work is extensive, and particularly if it affects all the key rooms – the kitchen, bathroom and toilets – it will be much less stressful and more comfortable if you can afford to move out for most of the building programme. If there is not enough in your budget, or you are concerned about security, or it would prove inconvenient in some other way, you will need to plan the programme of work carefully and will need a sympathetic builder. In most cases, it is possible to rig up basic facilities, or phase the work to keep a minimum number of rooms available to live in.

A useful tool for monitoring progress of the building work and predicting the timing and scale of disruption you are going to experience is a programming chart. Your builder may produce one of these without prompting. Alternatively, there may be one that he would prefer not to issue to you – because you can use it keep a close eye on how he is progressing. It should be readily available because no competent builder would start anything other than the very simplest project without one.

Hot Tip

Regardless of what the builder says, always allow for at least a 20 per cent overrun on the completion date, and have a contingency plan if it is longer – but keep this to yourself. If you are building or managing the project yourself instead of a contractor, allow for a 50 per cent overrun and have a contingency plan if you run completely out of time or enthusiasm or find you have less skill at building than you believe.

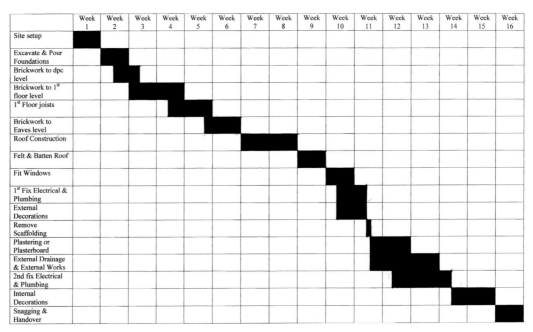

A typical programme for a small, two-storey extension. Author.

Insist that you are given a copy, before work starts on site, preferably before the contract is signed.

PRE-CONTRACT MEETING

Before a contractor occupies the site, it is a good idea to have a meeting to discuss the way that the project is to be run, which can be combined with the signing of the contract. It is important that you are re-assured that this project, which is to be run in your name, will be well managed, and will cause as little inconvenience to your neighbours as possible. Most important of all, the site must be as safe as possible. The builder, agent (such as the architect, if there is one) and client should all be represented.

The best-run projects are based on good communication between all parties, and this is the time to arrange some regular project meetings,

---

Standard Agenda for Pre-Contract Meeting

1. Introductions. Full names and contact details of everyone, including mobile numbers and email addresses.
2. Contract.
   (a) Commencement and completion dates should be restated.
   (b) Programme. The contractor should be asked for a programme showing the dates by which key tasks will be completed. Typically this is prepared in the form of a bar chart.
   (c) The names, addresses and details of subcontractors to be used.
   (d) Insurance. Ask for photocopies of the relevant documents from the builder.
3. Local authority.
   (a) Planning approval. If it is needed, check it is in place and that any conditions have been satisfied. If it is not needed, check that confirmation of this has been received in writing from the local authority planning department.
   (b) Building regulations. Check that plans approval has been received and the building control officer will be notified that work is about to start.
4. Site.
   (a) Sign boards. Where will they be erected, if at all?
   (b) Storage. This can be a significant area so the location and restrictions should be agreed.
   (c) Extent of the working area.
   (d) Access. Where the workforce will park their cars (think of the neighbours) and how will they will get to and from the area of the work.
   (e) Working hours and whether late or weekend working is permissible.
5. Communications.
   (a) Contractor contact on site. Name and mobile phone number.
   (b) Client contact. Which member of your family is to be the main contact?
   (c) If there is an agent, note that instructions will be issued through them to the builder.
6. Information.
   (a) Information required. The contractor may need further drawings or specifications or decisions from you to progress the work.
   (b) Advance notice and dates should be agreed for the information needed.
   (c) Identify those elements of the work that need information from the contractor.
7. Payment.
   (a) Every four weeks or at agreed stages in the work.
   (b) Is there a contract administrator working for you and if so how will payment be authorized?
8. Health and safety.
   (a) What measures will the contractor have in place to manage health and safety?
   (b) Is the site easily accessible to children and other members of the general public, and will steps be taken to keep it safe and secure?
   (c) Who is directly responsible for health and safety within the builder's company?

Start a Site File

During construction, efficient management of information will be helpful. If you have not already done so, create a project file with the following sections for correspondence and notes:

- In the front, a sheet of contact details of everyone involved.
- Copy of contract documents.
- Site meetings.
- Client.
- Architect.
- Engineer.
- Contractor.
- Subcontractors.
- Planning department.
- Building control and regulations.
- Utilities – gas, water, drainage, electricity, telephones, IT.
- Suppliers and manufacturers.

---

where you should make notes and record important decisions in writing. You do not necessarily have to be present at all of them if you are using an architect to manage on your behalf, but in that case make sure that you are kept informed of all the important discussions.

At the end of the pre-contract meeting, you should have all the information necessary to form the basis of a detailed contract. Often the signing happens on the day but sometimes there is a short delay whilst some issues raised are resolved. For a detailed look at building contracts and their implications, see Chapter 10.

CONTRACT MANAGEMENT MEETINGS

Throughout the building programme, there will be frequent informal meetings, between you and the builder and possibly others, such as the architect, building control officer and subcontractors. Always ensure that someone keeps a written note of these discussions and, ideally, issues copies to anyone involved or affected. It is very easy for people to walk away with a different idea of what

has been agreed, but if a note is sent, it will avoid the problems that can result from this common type of misunderstanding. Also it is sometimes very difficult to remember exactly who said what and when a few weeks after the event. In addition to these 'ad hoc' meetings, there should be more formal meetings, with dates agreed in advance and all the relevant members of your team present. Your architect or builder may organize these, but if you are project managing, it will be your responsibility.

All builders should keep a site diary, where deliveries, visits to site, instructions, workmen present and so on, should all be recorded; some do not bother. You should certainly keep your own diary, possibly in the form of a loose-leaf ring binder, so that you have a chronological record of all the important events and decisions made on site.

These planned meetings are essential to the smooth running of the project and it is vital that there is a standard agenda and that someone takes notes and issues them afterwards. A standard agenda ensures that important issues are not forgotten. Sometimes what is not said is as important as the actual discussions. For example, if you have an agenda item called 'progress', and a point in the meeting notes where the weather is

---

Standard Agenda for a Regular Progress Meeting

1. Present and apologies.
2. Weather and site conditions.
3. Stage of the works as observed on site.
4. Progress and contractor's report on programme.
5. Contractor's report.
6. Information required.
7. Client's matters.
8. Confirmation of new instructions.
9. Confirmation of any extra costs.
10. Site-inspection matters.
11. Date and attendance for next meeting.

You can create your own agenda, as long as it covers the issues stated above and is used as a checklist at each meeting.

---

recorded, this gives the builder the opportunity to state if he is behind programme and also note if bad weather has delayed the project. Provided it is a standard item, the notes will record 'nothing to report', which can be used later if the builder was to suggest that the programme has slipped because of heavy rain before the time of the meeting, when it fact it is due to slow progress later in the project.

HEALTH AND SAFETY ON SITE

A building site is one of the most dangerous places to work. In turn, the most dangerous place on a building site is at high level. There are many deaths and countless injuries related to people falling from a height or things being dropped on to them from above. It is essential that any builder or trades-man who works on your property complies with current health and safety requirements.

The sad truth is that you may well find that some or all of the rules listed in the box (see next page) are blatantly ignored by your builders. This is the main reason that hospital casualty departments are kept so busy by the construction industry. If the health and safety rules are not followed, money is saved and it may be that part of the benefit is passed on to you as the customer. But before you shut your eyes to the increased risk of accidents, think about the possible consequences for your family. If that is not enough to worry you, think about the risk that you will run if the health and safety inspector decides that you are criminally responsible if someone else is injured or killed on your property.

If you do not use a single contractor to carry out all the work, it is possible that you will be deemed to be at least partly responsible should any acci-dents occur whilst building. Since it is potentially a crime, subject to prosecution and fines, you should ensure either that you do not take this responsi-bility by appointing a professional, or that you are fully familiar with the regulations and competent to enforce them. You will have a duty to the people that you hire to do the work, but also to members of the public and others who may visit the site, such as a postman, family or friends.

Fortunately, in the UK, the Health and Safety Executive produce a wide range of advisory book-lets and leaflets. They are comprehensive and many are free, so there is no excuse for not knowing the necessary precautions.

ABOVE: **The most dangerous place on a building site is at high level.**

BELOW: **If there is access to the site from a public road, is there a secure fence with warning signs?**

Health and Safety Checklist

This list is not exhaustive and is no substitute for researching the duties imposed by the Health and Safety Executive and the regulations. If the rules are being properly followed, everyone should be wearing a hard hat, steel toe-cap boots and a high visibility jacket, otherwise known as personal protective equipment, or PPE. This applies to the workforce, any visitors to the site such as building control officers and you and your family.

Access To and Around the Site
Common accidents: road accidents as vehicles leave the site or people falling into foundation trenches that have not been fenced off or clearly marked.

Is the site tidy?
Are all excavations and holes marked and protected?
Is access for vehicles safe and well marked?

Scaffolding
Common accidents: tools rolling off and falling on to heads below or extra loads making the scaffold unstable.

Has it been erected by specialists, who inspect it regularly?
Are all the edges of the boards protected with upstands to prevent tools rolling off?
Are there guard rails to prevent people falling off?
Is the scaffold well-secured to the building?
What is the limit of loads, such as piles of bricks and tiles?
Are there barriers and warning notices to prevent misuse in the evenings and weekends?

Ladders
Common accident: the top of the ladder sliding off whilst someone is climbing up; falling from ladders counts for up to a quarter of injuries on construction sites.

Are they in sound condition, suitable for the heavy duty purpose?

Are they securely tied at the top, to a solid surface?
Does the top of the ladder extend beyond the level it reaches (so that it can be held on to when climbing on and off?

Excavations
Common accidents: sides falling in and crushing the person in the trench, people falling into the trench, adjoining buildings collapsing.
Is the trench properly supported to prevent it caving in?
Is there safe access into and out of the trench?
If it is a deep trench, is there protection around the edge to prevent anyone falling in?
Has the depth of foundations and stability of existing buildings nearby been checked?

Manual Handling
Common accidents: back injuries from lifting incorrectly or loads that are too heavy.

Where there are heavy materials to be moved by hand, can they be broken down into safe loads or moved with a wheelbarrow instead?
Is everyone working on the site aware of how to correctly lift heavy loads?
Is appropriate machinery available to carry loads that are too heavy for safe lifting and carrying by the workforce?

Vehicles and Plant
Common accidents: unstable plant toppling when loaded or vehicles reversing into objects and people.

Do the vehicles work properly and are they properly serviced?
Are the drivers trained for the plant that they are operating?
Have the acceptable gradients on which the machines will remain stable been checked?

Hoists, Cranes and Lifts

Common accident: load falling from the hoist whilst in transit.

Have the people using them been trained to do so?

Is the maximum permissible load clear?

Has the equipment been regularly checked to ensure it is in good condition?

Emergencies

Common accident: a minor injury becomes more serious because it cannot be treated until help arrives or the person is taken to hospital because there is no first aid treatment on site.

Does everyone know what to do if there is an emergency such as a fire?

How will the alarm be raised?

Is there a first aid box with all the necessary contents in an obvious place?

Hazardous Substances

Common accidents: burns from contact with wet concrete or inhalation of noxious fumes.

Are all hazardous substances identified clearly when they arrive on site?

If the presence of asbestos is suspected, has a survey been carried out by a licensed contractor?

Is there any way of using a non-hazardous substance instead?

Are workers trained to avoid the risks and able to identify the symptoms of any potential harm occurring?

Are there procedures to prevent workers being alone when using hazardous substances?

Noise

Common accidents: many older construction workers suffer from deafness or tinnitus brought about by excessive noise on site and experiences much earlier in their working life.

Have workers been trained in the risk of noise and how to reduce them?

Can the noise be reduced by using different machinery or maintenance?

Are ear defenders available for all workers in noisy situations?

Hand/Arm Vibration

Common accidents: hand arm vibration syndrome, (HAVS), otherwise known as vibration white finger, typically causing numbness, pain and restricted use of hands, resulting from prolonged use of vibrating hand-held machinery.

Have workers been trained in the risks of HAVS and how to avoid them?

Have steps been taken to reduce the likelihood of workers being put at risk?

Are the tools properly maintained?

Electricity and Services

Common accidents: electrocution caused by severing a buried mains cable during excavation work or unidentified live wires around the partly constructed building.

Have all services been identified and made safe before work commences?

Can low voltage battery-operated tools be used, in preference to mains powered?

Are cables and leads protected from damage?

Have the site and tools been checked for electrical safety by a competent person?

Public and Other Visitors to the Site

Common accident: children get on to the site and are injured or killed because they do not appreciate the danger that they are in.

Is the work fenced off from the public highway and are warning signs in place?

Is the site made secure after work finishes at the end of the day?

Are all ladders allowing access to higher areas removed and made secure?

Is the site left safe in the event of unexpected weather conditions, e.g. high winds?

Personal Protection

Common accidents: head and foot injuries from falling objects.

TYPICAL REAR EXTENSION WITH LOFT CONVERSION

TOP LEFT: **The existing house.**

TOP RIGHT: **Demolition and creation of the foundations begins.**

MIDDLE LEFT: **The first lift of the brickwork almost complete.**

MIDDLE RIGHT: **Completed extension and dormer window for the loft conversion.**

BOTTOM LEFT: **The completed interior.**

CERTIFICATES

Broadly speaking, certificates are written statements that either require something to be done (such as payment), state that something has been done properly or guarantee an aspect of the work. The certificate is only as good as the authority of the person signing it and the organization by which it is backed. There are several types of certificate that you may need for the work on your project.

JULIAN OWEN ASSOCIATES
ARCHITECTS

276 Queens Road
Beeston, Nottingham
NG9 2BD

t 0115 922 9831
f 0115 922 4616
e enquiries@julianowen.co.uk

www.julianowen.co.uk

Issued by: Julian Owen Associates Architects

Employers: Mr K Colyer
Address: 23 Back to the Delta Avenue, Old Riley, Nottingham NG51 2NO

Contractor: K C Jones Building Contractors
Address: 80 Grey Goose Street, Old Hannah, Notts, NG81 5QP

Interim Certificate

Works: New Side Extension and Swimming Pool
Situated at: Private house, adjacent to Muleskinner Pub, Riley Road, Ellaspeed, Notts, NG56 0LD

Start on Site: 17th December 2007

Job Ref: 1200

Certificate No: 9

Issue Date: 25.03.11

Valuation Date: 27.02.11

Contract Sum: £166,570.00

We certify that, under the terms of the above mentioned contract, payment is due from the Employer to the Contractor as detailed below:

£

Total Value of the Works:.......... 165,921.30

Less Retention of 5%................. 8,296.07

Balance...................................... 157,625.23

Less Total Previously Certified.. 139,903.65

Net Amount for Payment........... 17,721.58

In Words: Seventeen Thousand Seven Hundred and Twenty One Pounds and Fifty Eight Pence

All Amounts Exclusive of VAT

Signed: _____   Date: 25.03.09

(On Behalf of Julian Owen Associates Architects)

An Interim Certificate that approved payment to the builder. It must be honoured within seven days.

Distribution	Original to:	Copies to:		
	[*] Employer	[*] Contractor	[ ] Engineer	[*] File
		[ ] Sub Contractor	[ ] Quantity S	[ ]

JOAA2003

This is not a Tax Invoice

Interim Certificates

If an architect or contract administrator is being used to run the project for you on a day-to-day basis, the contractor is usually paid by you after the architect has checked that the amount being claimed is due. A small amount of the money due is retained, usually 5 per cent. These certificates do not mean that the building work has been 'approved', just that the architect thinks that it is reasonable to make the payment taking into account the work that has been completed. If you are not using an architect, and the project if of significant size, it is a good idea to agree a similar arrangement with your builder in advance. Either payment is made at set intervals of time (e.g. every month) based on the work completed, or you agree amounts in advance tied into stages of work as they are reached.

Practical Completion Certificates

An architect issues this certificate when the work is virtually finished and usually is ready to be used by your family. There is sometimes pressure for practical completion to be certified before all the work is done, so that the rooms can be occupied. If this is done, a list of defects and uncompleted work should be agreed with the builder. It is not generally considered good practice because it reduces the pressure on the contractor to finish, but is usually acceptable as long as the list is not lengthy. At this point, half the 5 per cent retention is released.

Final Certificate

Of the retention, 2.5 per cent is held back for six or twelve months and the building is then re-inspected by the architect. This usually results in a list of minor defects that need to be fixed by the builder before the architect issues the Final Certificate and requires you to pay the retention.

Building Control/Approved Inspector Completion Certificates

Building Control and their private equivalent, Approved Inspectors, usually issue a Full Plans certificate once they have checked the drawings, calculations and specifications before works starts. They can also issue a certificate of completion at the end of the building work if asked to do so. This certificate can be important when the building is sold, or if a VAT reclaim is to be made (e.g. if the project is a conversion into a domestic house).

Manufacturer's and Supplier's Guarantees

It is worth getting any certificates issued by suppliers and manufacturers that guarantee their products, because they are usually free and at least show that the correct products have been used; but they are often of limited value. They tend to have a number of 'get out' clauses such as stating that all their recommendations have to be followed by the builder in order for the guarantee to be valid – but the most common cause of failure is when these have not been complied with. The primary responsibility still lies with the builders, and unless you can get the guarantee in your name, you will still have to go to them to get something put right. Guarantees of up to thirty years are only valid for as long as the company that issues them is in business, unless they are with a third-party insurer, which is rare.

RISK ANALYSIS – ANTICIPATING PROBLEMS AND HOW TO PREVENT THEM

All one-off building projects have risks associated with them and yours will be no different. The key to avoiding risks is to recognize that they may happen and either have a strategy for avoiding them altogether, or know how to work out what you will do if they happen. You should also categorize the risk in terms of the likelihood that they will happen and the severity of the consequences if they do. For example, the chances of the brick type you have specified being unavailable are probably quite low, but even if this happened, finding a different one would be fairly easy and have little consequence to most projects. Conversely, there is quite a high risk of theft on building sites, and the consequences could be significant. An example of a risk in between these extremes is something that is unlikely to happen but if it does will have serious consequences, such as the discovery of an unknown public drain as the foundations are exca-

Risk Assessment Table			
	Low Risk 1	Medium Risk 2	High Risk 3
Little Consequence 1	2	3	4
Medium Consequence 2	3	4	5
Severe Consequence 3	4	5	6

This table can be applied to each risk, eventually giving all of them a ranking. If a risk scores 6, it is essential to avoid it or have proper contingencies in place as soon as possible.

vated for a new extension. This is unlikely if you do your homework properly, but the effect might be that nothing can be built and the project has to be abandoned. By examining the risks in this way, you can set priorities and decide how much trouble you will take to avoid them. If you want to be scientific about it, you can use a standard table like the one shown above. The higher a risk scored on this table, the more important it is to avoid.

Going Over Budget

This is the biggest risk for any project, partly because it is very difficult to estimate prices accurately before detailed drawings have been prepared.

How to Reduce the Risks

- Get professional advice during the design stage.
- Set a contingency of 10–15 per cent before design work starts.
- Ensure that a thorough set of drawings is prepared for pricing.
- Agree a fixed-price quotation for the building work, not an approximate estimate.
- Investigate the existing building thoroughly.
- Don't change your mind after the price has been agreed.
- Don't allow the builder to do extra work without agreeing a price first.

Planners Identify Problems on Site

It is usual for planning conditions to be discharged before 'development commences' or 'occupation'.

The new work must comply with the approved drawings.

How to Reduce the Risks

- Ensure that you get a full copy of the planning approval notice and that the builder also has a copy.
- Read it carefully before work starts.
- Get approval of conditions in writing.
- Check that the working drawings to be used by the builder match the approved drawings.
- If there are contentious issues, make sure the builder knows about them, for example if the ridge of the roof must not be over a certain height.
- If the building or the site is an irregular shape or there are level changes, have an accurate survey carried out by a specialist surveyor before design work starts.

Poor-Quality Workmanship or Poor-Quality Materials

- The savings made by commissioning poorly built construction work will be outweighed by the cost of remedial work needed later and the reduced value of the property.
- Choose the right builder to suit your own standards. Cheap is not the same as good value.
- Allow enough money in your budget for the quality you expect before the design process starts.

- Employ an architect to inspect and certify the building work.
- Only pay after work has been completed and withhold money if the work is not up to standard.
- Be realistic: if you want perfection you should be prepared to pay extra for it.
- Specify the required standards, e.g. NHBC, the relevant British Standards, Agrément Certificates.

Delay

If the building work takes a lot longer than planned, it can increase the cost of finance of the project, as well as rental or mortgage costs if you move out for the duration. There is also a psychological cost in stress and uncertainty.

How to Reduce the Risks

- Agree a realistic fixed date for completion with the builder as a contract condition.
- Don't apply pressure for the builder to agree to an unrealistic timetable.
- Ensure that the building work is described in sufficient detail.
- Include a clause that allows you to deduct money for delay that is the fault of the contractor (liquidated damages).
- Release payment to the builder at pre-agreed stages in the work, such as damp proof course level or completion of brickwork, rather than regular time-related payments (e.g. every four weeks).
- Allow for the work to overrun on your own programme, but don't tell the contractor.
- Don't make significant changes on site, especially after the work has been carried out.

Unexpected Ground Conditions

Difficult ground conditions can be expensive and so need to be built into the budget at an early stage. Sometimes it is impossible to check every part of the ground that will be built upon, but you can do a lot to greatly reduce the risk of hitting unexpected problems.

Poor ground can be identified very early on. Badly drained, heavy clay will easily squeeze into a ball in your hand.

How to Reduce the Risks

- Dig trial holes to check the existing foundations and the ground close to the area of any new extension. Don't disturb the ground where the foundations are actually going to go, if possible.
- Talk to neighbours who have had extensions built to find out if they had problems.
- Check with the local authority building control officers. They know the ground conditions of their 'patch' well.
- Check the existing buildings in the area for signs of structural cracking.
- Be particularly careful if your house is on a steep slope, where it is common for some of the land to be poorly-consolidated filled ground.

Building Set Out Incorrectly

If the building does not fit on the site correctly because it is too large or the wrong shape, it can lead to problems with the planning department and neighbours.

How to Reduce the Risks

- Get a detailed, accurate, professional survey carried out before design work starts. If there are lots of level changes or irregular plan shapes, use a specialist surveyor.

- Ensure that the builder checks all the dimensions on site before laying foundations. This should be a contractual requirement.
- Don't assume that walls are parallel or rectilinear just because they look like it, especially if the building is very old.
- If you are using old, existing plans, prepared by others, don't assume that they are all correct.
- Some builders don't follow the plans they have been issued with correctly, so key dimensions should be discretely checked on site by someone else.

Drawings are Incorrect

If the drawings are significantly wrong and it is only discovered as the work is constructed, this can cause serious problems and cost.

How to Reduce the Risks

- Use a qualified professional with a proven track record, who can visualize the project in three dimensions.
- Ensure that whoever does the drawings will treat it as an important project, not a 'fill-in' between larger projects.
- Make sure that the drawings are of a sufficiently large scale to identify all the tricky areas of the construction. 1:50 scale sections are fine for building regulations application, but leave a lot to be worked out by the builder on site and do not show the construction in great detail. Sometimes at least a 1:20 section is required and maybe 1:5 details as well.
- Make sure that crucial points around the building are double checked, e.g. staircase clearances, distances from boundaries, overall building height.

Fire and Theft

The losses from a disaster can be significant.

How to Reduce the Risks

- Notify your insurers that building work is about to start, and disclose full details of the project.

- Make sure that your house insurance is compatible with the builder's insurance provision.
- Ask for proof that insurance is in place from the contractor in the form of copies of the relevant documents.
- Check that the contractor is properly securing the site, especially if you are not present when they leave, and over weekends.
- Consider including a requirement to provide a separate alarm system for the area of the building work.
- If you have any of your own property within the area of the building work, move it to somewhere more secure and lockable.

Someone Gets Hurt

Death and injury are significant risks on a building site. Many accidents are avoidable but result from people not following very basic common sense safety rules.

How to Reduce the Risks

- Make compliance with current health and safety legislation a condition of your contract with the builder.
- If you have young children, ensure that they never have the opportunity to get into the areas of building work unaccompanied.
- Resist the temptation to take your family on a tour of the work until it is well on the way to completion and safer to enter.
- If the contractor is not complying with obvious safety procedures, insist that they do so. If they will not cooperate, you are within your rights to issue a warning that you will inform the Health and Safety Executive.
- Check that ladders are not left in position and openings have been blocked off before the workforce leave the site on evenings and weekends.
- Never go on to scaffolding or climb up high around the works unless the builder is present and has confirmed that it is safe for you to do so.

Unreasonable Expectations

Sometimes relations between a builder and client break down because the homeowner expects the builder to achieve standards that they are incapable of satisfying.

How to Reduce the Risks

- If you have high standards, allow more in the budget to pay for them.
- Send out for tenders from builders who you are sure will all work to a similar standard.
- If you are looking for a higher standard than average, indicate this when you invite tenders.
- Show the builder an existing building or part of a building that has been built to the standard you require, if possible.
- If there are aspects of the work that require a much higher standard that the rest of the building, select your own specialists and instruct the builder to use them (e.g. stonemasons, decorators).
- If you are unhappy with something that has been built, talk to the builder and not the workman. Explain your concerns in a tactful manner.
- When the workforce has left the site, never go around the building leaving notes criticizing the work, ready to be found when they arrive back in the morning.

Contractor Goes Bankrupt

Insolvency is an unfortunate possibility for any building contractor, and smaller firms are particularly vulnerable. If it happens in the middle of your project, it will probably cost you money to get your project back on course.

How to Reduce the Risks

- Before you appoint a builder run a financial check. This is easy to do on the internet (e.g. www.companieshouse.gov.uk or www.experian.co.uk).
- Agree fair payment terms, but do not pay for anything in advance unless the builder will, in turn, have to pay up front. The latter is rare in the UK building industry.

- Keep a retention out of any payment due until the work is completed, e.g. 5 per cent. This is accepted practice in the industry and most builders should agree to it.
- Check that there is a clause in the contract that states some rules as to what you can do if the builder goes into administration.
- Look for signs of unpaid bills, e.g. sudden changes in suppliers, subcontractors or builders' merchant.
- Never pay a subcontractor directly if they come to you complaining that they have not been paid by the builder.
- If the contractor does go into administration, secure the site immediately and do not let anyone on to it, including the builder, unless you are present. Do not allow anyone to remove anything from site, even if they claim that they haven't been paid for it. Then seek professional advice as soon as possible.

You Fall Out with the Builder

If things go so badly that you find relations with your builder have broken down completely, bear in mind that the most likely result of him leaving site is that you will end up out of pocket.

How to Reduce the Risks

- Make sure you use a standard, written contract that clearly explains everything that you and the builder are obliged to do. Most disputes result from an unclear contract or one party failing to follow its stipulations.
- Know your obligations under the contract and make sure you keep to them, no matter what the provocation. Even if you think the builder in the wrong, should you breach the contract yourself this may absolve him of responsibility and make you the one who can be sued.
- Don't just prevent the builder from coming on to the site because you are unhappy with something, unless you have contract provisions that you can follow that allow you to do this.
- Get legal advice early, but try to avoid litigation if possible. It is rarely cost-effective except where very large sums are involved, although the small

claims route may be used if the amounts are below about £5,000.

- However bad it gets, try to keep talking to the builder. A dispute has little chance of being sorted out quickly once you have stopped speaking to each other.
- If it gets so bad that litigation seems your only option, look at mediation first – this is a process that tries to get both sides to compromise and avoid a costly legal battle.

REACHING COMPLETION

There are sometimes disagreements as to when a building project is complete, particularly when the payment of the last instalment is due. Completion is when everything that you have contracted the builder to do has been finished, and there are dangers in stretching the definition. Once the builder has most, if not all, of his money, it usually becomes difficult to get any outstanding minor defects fixed or incomplete work finished. The final payment should not be made until you are fully satisfied that the work is complete. If possible, you should put a clause into your contract that allows you to retain a small percentage of the total contract cost, typically 2.5 per cent for a six- or twelve-month period, in case there are any defects that come to light. JCT contracts include these provisions as standard. Contractors generally do not like the idea of retentions, but long experience shows that it can be very difficult to get defects fixed if there is no financial incentive.

On the day that completion has been agreed, carry out a tour of inspection of all the building work. Ideally you should do this unaccompanied, but if the builder insists on being there with you, do not allow yourself to be hurried. If you spot more than a few minor defects, stop the inspection and do not agree completion until the builder has properly snagged the work and had it corrected. Some builders prefer the client to carry out all the snagging of their team's work, on the basis that if you don't spot it, they can get away with it. This is unacceptable – it is not your job and you should only see very minor defects that can be remedied quickly. If you have an architect or similar profes-

Hot Tip

If you spot a snag, such as a badly hung door or a misaligned door latch, check all the other examples of the same feature. Often the problem is a particular workman, who may have got some or all the others wrong as well.

sional managing the contract, then you can leave a lot of this stage to them, but because it is your home, it is important that you are allowed to feed your comments into the process. As always, apply the test of reasonableness to your requirements. Sometimes it is impossible to get everything perfect, but on the other hand if something annoys you and is easy to correct, you should insist on it being put right.

Apart from ensuring that all the work is satisfactory, you should also ensure that you receive all the necessary certificates and guarantees that the builder is supposed to provide, such as the Building Control Completion Certificate, Gas Safe certificate, and so on. These must all be signed and issued by the appropriate people. If there is any doubt as to the qualifications of the issuers, this should be checked – something that can be done quite easily. When completion is agreed, it has a number of implications. You can occupy the space and start to live in it. At this stage the builder's insurance usually ceases to cover the areas of new work.

The other big question that usually has to be settled at this point is the final account. If your builder has been efficient and managed the project well, there should not be any nasty surprises. Any extra work should have been flagged up to you at the time it was agreed and the likely financial implications confirmed. Sometimes, either due to cunning or, more often, inefficiency, the builder presents a long and expensive list of extras that you are not expecting at the end of the job. If you have professional help in the form of an architect or other contract administrator, this should not be allowed to happen and they will have to sort it out

Snagging Checklist for Completion Stage

Pitched roof
Roof slates or tiles complete, undamaged, unmarked and properly bedded.
Vent tiles/eaves in place, fly screens fitted.
Are main edges, such as the ridge and line of the eaves, straight.
Flashings in place and properly fixed, with adequate lap and wedged into brickwork.
Ventilation openings adequate.

Rainwater drainage
Valley gutters are clean and free from debris.
Gutters and stop ends located correctly, sufficient brackets and falls in right directions.
Gutters clear of rubbish.
Roof underlay laps into gutter.

Brickwork
Pointing complete, gaps created by scaffolding made good.
Clean, no mortar splashes.
Mortar and brickwork consistent in colour.
Perpends line through neatly.
Weep holes above cavity trays, DPC and openings.

Downpipes
Fixed securely.
Locations match the drawings.

Overflow pipes
Visible.
Correct length.
Sealed at exit point.

Windows and external doors
No chips or splits or other damage.
Frames sealed at edges.
Glass clean and not scratched.
Beading securely fixed.

Paintwork and staining
Finished with all coats, especially where hidden, e.g. tops of doors, under window sills.

Ceilings
Corners are straight.

Paintwork
All coats of paints applied.
Free from patches.
Cleaned down.
Smooth surface, free of plasterboard joints, popped nail heads and cracks.

Plasterwork
Smooth, even surfaces.
Gaps made good around service penetrations.
Junctions and corners straight.

Windows internally
Painted properly.
Timberwork undamaged.
No scratches or marks on the glass.
Open and close smoothly.
No distortion in the frame.
Trickle ventilators working.
Compliance with escape requirements on first floor and above.
Window locks and keys available (if specified).

Doors internally
Painted properly
Timberwork undamaged.
Open and shut when handle turned.
Latches are secure, i.e. doors do not pull open without turning the handle.
No distortion or twisting in the frame.
Door has an equal gap around the frame.
Ironmongery and locks clean and as specified and locks area working properly.

Skirtings and architraves
Level, with clean line along the top.
Undamaged with no dents or marks and painted properly.

Floor finishes
Tiling complete, even, regularly spaced and sealed at joints.

Vinyl smooth and even with no bubbles or lumps.

Clean.

Timber board surface floor smooth, clean and ready for carpet, etc.

No creaks (these will always gradually get worse if not picked up early).

Services

Pipes supported with plenty of clips.

Radiators securely fixed, clean, with bleed points accessible.

Switches and sockets clean, level and secure.

Staircases

Ballustrading, newels, handrails securely fixed.

Surface varnish or paint complete, clean and undamaged.

Equal risers and goings.

Bathrooms

All fittings clean, working and without chips or blemishes.

Taps working.

Toilets flush.

Plugs and other attachments present.

No leaks to plumbing.

Worktop unblemished.

Cupboard doors fitted square and secure.

Plumbing

No leaks.

Pipework securely fixed.

No airlocks in pipe bends.

Electrical

All fitted appliances working (e.g. cooker, heaters).

Mechanical ventilation working.

Gas and fires

Appliances operation properly.

Ventilation available as required by building regulations.

for you if it does. If you are on your own, the position is tricky, because technically, if you have agreed that the builder should carry out extra work, and you have had the benefit of it, you will probably have to pay up. The problem is in deciding how much, because the builder's price may seem unreasonably high.

It is not unusual for a builder to charge more for extra work needed once the work has started than it would have cost if had it been included in the tender. Somehow you will have to agree what is a reasonable charge, in retrospect. In the first instance it is incumbent on the builder to show that the price is fair. If you doubt the figure, it is perfectly reasonable to ask to see actual invoices for materials and even timesheets (sometimes called 'dayworks' sheets) or a site diary, along with a statement of how long the individual workmen spent doing the tasks involved, on what days they worked and how much each is being paid. There is no reason for the builder to claim confidentiality and refuse to show these records to you. The records should be available if the company is being run in an honest and professional manner. If the contractor establishes that the work is genuinely an extra that you agreed to at the time, and can show that the price is reasonable, payment is legitimately due. As usual, a great deal of argument can be avoided by having a proper contract that sets out the rules for what happens in these situations.

There is a danger in getting too obsessed with the detail of a final account and spending hours scrutinizing each extra and omission. However, if your builder has dealt with you in an open, honest manner throughout the project, has worked diligently and produced good-quality work, it may be more reasonable to take a step back and consider whether, as a whole, you have had good value for money. If the builder has not put in a claim for every single minor extra, it is churlish to try to create savings from minor omissions. If the builder has done the job well, you might consider accepting that, overall, you have had good value for money and pay what is being claimed. Producing good building work at a fair price takes skill and dedication and deserves fair payment.

At the end of the building work check for defects carefully, because it is much easier to get them put right before the builder is paid and leaves the site. This socket is out of level and should be re-fixed.

If you have got good value and the project has been done to a high standard, appreciate the effort that has been made on your behalf. If you can afford it, consider paying a small bonus.

Before you let the contractor leave the site, ask for all the documents that will help you and future owners maintain the building, covering aspects such as:

- Heating.
- Alarm system.
- Appliances.
- Electrical layout and fittings.
- As built drawings.

Also make sure that you have the names and addresses of all the key suppliers and subcontractors, some of whom may agree to come back for routine maintenance.

You also need to be sure that all the necessary approvals and certificates are in place, along with any suppliers/manufacturer's guarantees, such as:

- Building Regulations Certificate (may be sent to you directly from the council).
- Gas appliances certified under the Capita Gas Registration and Ancillary Services Limited scheme (formerly CORGI), known as 'Gas Safe'.
- Electrical work certified under the EC Certification Limited certification process (formerly Electrical Contractors Association).
- Guarantees from suppliers of appliances.
- Guarantees from suppliers of laminate and other specialist floors.
- Warranties for any specialist features or components, such as a built-in home cinema.

CHAPTER 10

Legal Issues

Things You Should Know About Before Starting Your Project

1. Your rights as a consumer.
2. How contract law works.
3. Contracts with builders and professional advisors.
4. Insurance requirements.
5. The Party Wall Act, and if it applies.

CONSUMER RIGHTS

There is a certain kind of legislation that is designed to add extra terms to a contract between a consumer and a supplier of products. These are called 'implied terms' and automatically apply to a contract, even if they are not discussed or written into it. Some of the laws apply to you agreeing contracts for work on your house in a different way than to a building professional, like a developer or business. If the work is to your own, private home, you are deemed to be a 'consumer'. A 'consumer' is a natural person who is acting for their own personal purposes and has signed a contract in their own name.

There is a raft of legislation passed by the government over the years to give you protection from exploitation. Even if you consider yourself knowledgeable on legal or building matters, the law deems you to be a consumer and assumes that you do not have the same level of skill and experience as the building professionals that you engage. The consumer laws are designed to redress the balance

and give you the advantage in the face of any unreasonable contract terms and also places the onus on the other party to explain what the contract means, as well as preventing unscrupulous terms being included in the small print. Some of your rights are enshrined in the law and will override anything that the signed contract says. These are the same type of laws that protect you if you go into a shop and buy something, or purchase a holiday.

Consumers are also exempt from some laws that place obligations or restrictions on professional developers and builders. The way that you are identified in these laws is usually as someone who is having work carried out on their own home, so if you are a landlord or paying for the work through your business, you will be subject to the extra requirements.

The Unfair Terms in Consumer Contracts Regulations 1999

These regulations recognize that you do not have specialist knowledge of the design and construction process, and place the onus on the people that you employ to explain the implications of the contract. In a contract between two parties, neither of whom is a consumer, even highly unreasonable terms are difficult to omit because the law assumes that both sides are fully aware of the legal implications of all the contractual terms (however wrong that assumption may be). A key provision in the unfair terms legislations is to give the courts the power to strike out an unreasonable term in a standard contract, unless it was specifically raised with you before you signed up and its full impli-

---

Laws That Do Not Apply to People Having Work Carried Out to Their Own Home

Part 8 of the Local Democracy, Economic Development and Construction Act 2009
This has provisions that prevent one party from not paying another unless they serve notice in advance and that allow either party to instigate an adjudication process if there is a dispute.

The Construction (Design and Management) Regulations 2007
Sometimes called the 'CDM Regs', these regulations make it compulsory for the developer to hire a health and safety manager for a project, from before the design work starts until the end of the construction. Most of the requirements do not apply to private house projects, although all the usual health and safety requirements for running a building site must be complied with by the builder and designer.

Late Payment of Commercial Debts (Interest) Regulations 2002
These deal with interest that can be claimed if a business is late paying a debt.
Important Note: Some of the rules laid out by the above legislation are written into the contract as express terms. If this is done they may be enforceable under contract law. In a commercial contract, they apply even if they are not mentioned in the contract.

---

cations explained. This means that if a contractor or architect tries to smuggle an unfair requirement into the small print of a contract without your knowledge, they will not be able to enforce it. A term is defined as unfair if it is 'contrary to the requirement of good faith, it causes a significant imbalance in the parties' rights and obligations arising under the contract, to the detriment of the consumer'. The legislation applies to any company that is involved in work to your home who either supplies and fits good, supplies goods only or fits only

So, you should always read the small print, and if anything is unclear insist that it is explained to you. But if you miss clauses, such as those requiring you to pay for everything in advance or removing your right to cancel the contract if any services are unsatisfactory, this legislation means that you are not obliged to comply with them.

If a professional fails to draw the attention of their potential clients to their terms and conditions, or makes them difficult to read or understand, this is a very bad omen for your future relationship with them. Good professionals will not want to enter into a contract with you unless they are sure that you fully understand the implications.

The Provision of Services Regulations 2009

This legislation applies to any person or company that provides a service to anyone, including to you as a consumer – in other words architects, builders, engineers, electricians and so on. It puts the onus on the service provider to fully inform the consumer of all the important information about the service being offered, such as the proper name and contact details of the company, who is in charge and even the qualifications of company employees, where relevant. It also requires that the service provider inform you how complaints may be handled. The best way for all this information to be provided is as part of the terms and conditions presented before you sign a contract, although the law does allow it to be held at the office until requested as long as it is 'easily accessible'.

Sale of Goods Act 1979 as Amended by the Sale and Supply of Goods to Consumers Regulations 2002

This very broad legislation includes construction-related goods – in other words, anything that you buy yourself to be incorporated in the work. There are three requirements. The first is that the goods must be 'of satisfactory quality' in the eyes of a typical, reasonable person, free from fault or defect, of reasonable appearance, safe and durable. They must be 'fit for purpose' and suitable for whatever use

---

Some Typical (Real Life) Unfair Terms That the Courts Will Strike Out

'We reserve the right to increase our prices during the course of the works and the client will be bound to pay any such increase when it becomes due.'

'All payment is due in advance of any building work commencing.'

'We accept no liability for any of the materials or goods supplied as part of this contract.'

'This contract cannot be cancelled by you at any time without our written agreement.'

'We will not be bound by any verbal agreements made on site.'

'In the event of you failing to pay us any amounts we deem to be due, the debt will be subject to an interest rate of 5 per cent per week.'

'We accept no responsibility for any loss, theft, injury, death or damage that occurs during the works, even if it is as a result of our own negligence.'

'All defects or work of unsatisfactory quality must be notified to us within 14 days in order for us to be liable to correct, replace or make good.'

'We do not accept any responsibility or liability for any delay to the work or related works whether due to circumstances under our control or other causes.'

'We fully guarantee the fixtures and fittings for a period of 6 months. Following this period any defects must be taken up directly with the manufacturers.'

'Should you cancel the work at any time prior to commencement, we reserve the right to retain any deposit and recover any consequent cost from you, plus any gross profit lost.'

'This contract may not be cancelled.'

'Final payment will become due when we consider that the work is complete.'

---

the supplier would expect at the time they were sold. The final main requirement is that they are 'as described'. This covers all descriptions of the goods, including anything stated by the supplier but not written down and any illustrations provided.

It effectively negates the wording on delivery forms that you are made to sign in the brief time before the delivery van leaves, which say that you have inspected the goods and they are satisfactory, when you have not even had time to open the box. If the goods are defective and you realize immediately, you are entitled to a refund. If you do not realize the defect and accept the goods, the supplier is obliged to replace them or carry out any repairs and bear all the costs of doing this. These rules apply for up to six years after the purchase and in some cases damages may be claimed.

The Consumer Protection (Distance Selling) Regulations 2000

These apply to any transactions that you make where you do not meet face-to-face with the other party, by telephone or the internet. They require the supplier to provide full details of the goods or services, including delivery arrangements, payment details, the full details of suppliers and any cancellation rights. The cancellation rights are usually in the form of a cooling-off period of seven working days. In other words, if you change your mind after the deal has been agreed, you have that time to cancel the order.

The Consumer Protection (Cancellation of Contracts Concluded Away from Business Premises) (Amendment) Regulations 1998

These regulations apply where someone has contacted you unbidden, either by appearing on your doorstep or as a result of a telephone call that was not requested, otherwise known as a 'cold call'. It also applies if you have contacted a company and invited them to your home for one type of goods or services but they sell you something else. This doesn't apply to financial transactions, land deals or goods or services less than £35. You have the right to a seven-day cooling-off period. If the trader doesn't provide written confirmation of the right to cancel, it is a criminal offence.

YOUR CONTRACT WITH YOUR PROFESSIONAL ADVISORS

If your designer is an architect, their registration body (Architects Registration Board) and the Royal Institute of British Architects (RIBA) require them to confirm their fees, appointment terms and scope of work in writing. The same requirements are true of members of the Chartered Institute of Architectural Technologists and Royal Institute of Chartered Surveyors. Some use standard appointment documents supplied by the professional bodies, but others will use their own version. A simple letter stating the fee is inadequate. If you don't have a crystal clear idea of what the professional is going to do for you, or exactly how the fees will be accrued, a dispute is likely to arise. Bear in mind that, apart from skill and experience, the main thing you are buying is their time spent on your project. If a fee is low, the consultant will have to reduce the amount of time spent, to make a profit. When this happens, opportunities are missed, details are skated over and problems are left unsolved for the builder to sort out on site. In short, a poor service from the designer will cost you far more than their fee to sort out later. In a few cases, dishonest consultants quote a very low fee and make their profit by taking secret commissions from builders and suppliers for getting them work on your project, which removes the competitive element from the tender process and allows the prices to be rigged. Unscrupulous builders will pay up to 10 per cent of the contract value if someone ensures that they get the job. Obviously, this is illegal and expensive for their clients, but it allows them to present attractively low fees for their services.

You should have a full copy of the agreement and you should also acknowledge your instruction to proceed in writing. This is not pointless bureaucracy. If you do not have a proper written agreement and anything goes wrong, you will find that the absence of agreed terms and conditions could prove a costly mistake.

Checklist for Items to Include in a contract with an Architect

A clear description of the work that the architect will be carrying out.

Who will issue the instructions on behalf of your family?

You should be clear who will appoint consultants, such as an engineer.

How fees will be worked out.

What items will be charged to you as expenses, such as mileage, and how much will they be?

At what intervals will invoices be issued and what are the payment terms?

If you are unhappy with something or have a query, which member of the senior management team can you go to?

What can you do if you wish to terminate the contract?

How can any disputes be settled between you?

Are the controlling directors or partners members of an organization that has professional standards, to whom you can complain, if necessary?

The reason that written agreements like this are essential is because they reduce the likelihood of any misunderstandings occurring, and ensure that you are clear about what the architect is going to be doing for you.

THE BUILDING CONTRACT

In its simplest form, a contract consists of an offer to do something from one party, acceptance by the other party and then some form of payments passing between them. A contract does not have to be written down to come into existence, but without clear written terms, the possibilities for confusion, deception and dispute are extensive. Before signing a building contract, it is worth appreciating the essential legal principles that will be in operation. The government passes new laws and the law changes over time, but in the UK often the interpretation of legal rights and who has transgressed them is a matter of judgement and opinion rather than a black and white issue. How the law is interpreted depends on what the last judge to consider the point in a court case decided, otherwise known as 'case law'. Consequently, the advice contained in this book is very general and should not be used as a basis for sorting out a specific legal issue. If there is any doubt consult a solicitor.

Some Definitions

There are definitions that it is useful to know when dealing with a building contract of any kind.

Quotation. A fixed price for the work that is to be carried out. To be effective, it has to be tied into a detailed description of the work, usually in the form of drawings and specifications. If this is not done, the builders are free to reduce the specifications should they wish to increase their profit. The ideal is to get a quotation for all the construction work, based on an accurate, thorough set of specifications and drawings. This is not always possible where an existing building is involved, because some aspects are unknown until the existing construction is exposed. However, the quoted price should not increase unless the builder can show that either you have changed your mind, or the extra work could not have reasonably been predicted when it was calculated.

Estimate. This is an approximation by the builder of the cost of the work. The price is not legally binding if you employ a builder based on an estimate. A contract based on an estimate carries a lot of risk for you, because once on site, the cost for the job can be increased significantly and, unless you can prove they are particularly unreasonable, you will be obliged to pay up.

Employer. Although you may be referred to as a 'client' or 'customer', in a strict legal sense, you are the employer under the contract. If you have a spouse, partner or someone else who wishes to take equal responsibility, they will be a joint employer if you both sign the contract, or if they are identified in it with your signature being 'on behalf of' yourself and the other person.

Contractor (sometimes called the 'main contractor'). This is whoever you employ directly to do building work for you, i.e. the builder. This includes people or companies that have specialist trades, such as plumbers, plasterers and electricians, who would otherwise be subcontractors if they fitted the description below.

Subcontractor. This is anyone who works on your house who is employed by the main contractor rather than directly by you. This does not include employees of the main contractor. For example, a plumbing subcontractor may be employed by a contractor who does not have these skills 'in house' on a fixed price, but a joiner may work for the builder as an employee with a weekly wage.

Agent. This is someone who is named in the contract as being able to issue instructions on your behalf. If you employ an architect to manage a project they are usually named as the agent or 'Contract Administrator'. There should only be one person or company named, and all your instructions should be issued by them, rather than by you.

Contract. This is a legal agreement, usually between two parties. In the UK, unless it involves the exchange of land, it does not have to be in writing. So, if you ask a builder to do a job for you after he has told you how much it will cost, you may have agreed a binding contract, even if there is no letter or contract confirming it. Because a verbal contract, by definition, has no permanent record, they can easily lead to disputes. Many disputes are caused unnecessarily because there is not enough detail in the written contract. A simple letter from the builder stating a price is inadequate for this type of project.

Party to a Contract. The employer or the contractor – you or the builder.

Guarantee. This means that if the building work that is the subject of the guarantee is substandard, you will be compensated in some way, usually with a payment or the work being put right at no cost. Guarantees are only as good as the company backing them, so an independent guarantee from a large insurer is valuable, but a thirty-year guarantee from a small limited company that could go into liquidation or be wound up well within that period, is worth little in the long term.

Variation. This is an aspect of the building work that is changed or added from what was agreed when the contract was signed. It may lead to an extra cost or a saving, or neither.

Agreeing the Building Contract

Never, ever, agree to engage a contractor for significant building work without a proper written contract from an independent source. It is not necessary to employ a solicitor to draft one especially for you – there are standard contracts available, some of which have been developed by committees with representatives from all the main bodies involved in the construction industry. This organization is called The Joint Contracts Tribunal or JCT. They are fair to all sides and are specifically designed to anticipate the most likely problems and stipulate how they should be dealt with. Do not use a contract prepared by the builder or on behalf of one of the contractor organizations, however keen the builder is for you to use it. Unsurprisingly, these tend to favour the contractor heavily

in comparison to the JCT and other independently prepared varieties. Unfortunately, a simple letter stating that the work will be done for a stated price is wholly inadequate in these litigation-obsessed times. If there is a lack of detail, it stacks the odds very heavily in favour of the contractor in the event of a dispute.

There are three main JCT contracts, available online or by ordering from most bookshops:

1. JCT Minor Works Building Contract. This contract is only appropriate if there is an architect or similar professional running the contract. You cannot use this contract without naming someone to act on your behalf in this way and it should never be used in any other circumstances; for example, nominating yourself as the contract administrator. It is really for larger projects, but can be used for relatively smaller jobs if necessary.

2. JCT Building Contract for a Home Owner/ Occupier. This excellent document is designed for a wide variety of domestic alterations and has an award from the Plain English Campaign. It comes in two varieties: one for use with an architect or

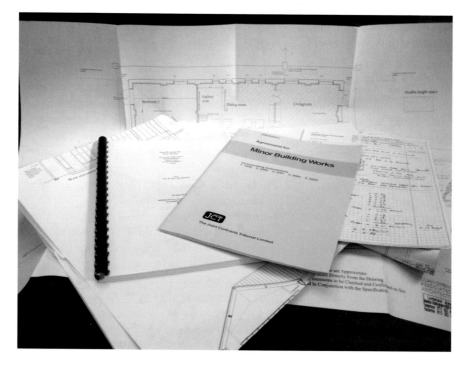

Always use a standard contract, readily available from bookshops and online, such as the JCT Minor Works Contract or JCT Contract for Home Owner/ Occupiers.

The Key Terms of a Building Contract

The following are some of the issues that should always be included in a building contract for a project of any size or complexity.

The Parties.   Who you are and the name of the builder. You may think this is obvious, but some builders have more than one company. And sometimes parties to contracts have used the fact that they have been wrongly described in a contract to avoid their liabilities.

The Identification of the Works.   A summary of the scope of the works, particularly important if the contractor takes on other work outside this contract, e.g. landscaping.

The Contract Documents.   It is essential to record the specific drawings, by number and revision letter, as well as the version of the specification. These may be different from the tender documents if there have been revisions to price since tenders were received.

Agent.   If you are using an architect or similar professional to manage the contract on your behalf, you must make clear what powers they have in the contract with the builders. You should also have a matching, separate written agreement with this agent.

The Tender Sum.   This has to tie in directly with the contract documents, and must reflect any post-tender changes. If it is a fixed price, this should be clearly and unambiguously stated.

The Project Duration and Liquidated Damages.   Many of the problems that arise between employer and builder are due to late completion of the work. The contract should state the time that work is to start, and when it is to be finished. A useful clause to have is one that states that any unwarranted delays will give you the right to make deductions from money due to the builder, usually a set amount for each week of overrun. These deductions are called 'liquidated damages'. This description means that they are set at a pre-agreed level and cannot be altered without the agreement of you and your builder, so you cannot ask for more that the stated figure. The amount of liquidated damages must be a reasonable calculation of the expected costs – if you pick a very high figure as an incentive to the builder to finish on time, the courts will not enforce it. Liquidated damages are sometimes wrongly referred to as 'penalties'.

Payment Terms.   Contractors are usually paid every four weeks, or at specific stages in the job, e.g. external shell completed to make the roof watertight again. Also a small amount should be held back until the end of the job, usually 5 per cent. A smaller amount should be kept until six months after work is finished (usually 2.5 per cent). These are all standard requirements in typical building contracts used in the UK construction industry.

Variations.   These are items of the work that are omitted, changed or added after the contract has been signed.

Insurance.   The contractor must have, and maintain, adequate insurance, but this may not be extended to cover items that belong exclusively to you and are stored on site, unless you ask for it. It is essential to talk to your own insurers and tell them the details of the contract before the work starts, and ensure that there are no gaps between the cover that the builder holds and your own.

Solving Disputes.   There should be a description of what parties can do if there is a dispute, and what to do if it cannot be settled.

similar consultant, and one for use without this assistance. It includes all the essential requirements of a building contract, but does not deal with some of the problems that may arise with larger sized projects; for example, there is no way of deducting money if the contractor overruns the agreed date for completion.

3.   JCT Contract for Home Repairs and Maintenance. This is for very small-scale repairs or building works. It allows for an hourly rate to be paid or a lump sum, and for only one payment at the end of the project. It is not recommended for work that is likely to take more than a month to complete.

On signing the contract, the employer (you) takes on certain duties, mainly concerned with payment, but also takes the ultimate responsibility and risk for the contract. Much of the management work can be delegated to an architect, if you choose to employ one to help on site. In this respect, having work done to your home is very different from buying a house from a developer and being simply 'a customer'. After you have signed a contract, and everyone is clear about their responsibilities, it can be put away, and hopefully there will be no need to refer to it again. But if there is a dispute, it will give you much more security and a good chance of resolving the problem without resorting to lengthy and expensive legal action.

WHAT TO DO IF YOU ARE IN DISPUTE WITH YOUR BUILDER

If at all possible, it is better to try to reach a reasonable compromise with the other party with whom you are in dispute rather than get tied up in a lengthy legal battle. This is because the legal system in the UK can be very expensive and it is rarely good sense for either side to get as far as the courts, particularly if the amount is relatively small. For example, £10,000 or £20,000 may seem a lot to you, but in legal terms this may not be considered worth pursing when set alongside the costs of hiring a solicitor, barrister and paying court fees. There are plenty of examples of court cases being pursued because a personal battle has developed between the two parties who become locked into a struggle to prove the other side wrong that may take years to reach a conclusion.

After you have tried and failed negotiating a resolution yourself, you will need to get independent advice, from an independent construction professional or solicitor. People who have not experienced the legal process are often surprised to find that it does not decide who has behaved well and who badly, or even who is 'right' and who is 'wrong'. What actually happens is that the courts decide who has the law on their side. This means that it is possible for someone to behave in an unreasonable manner, but if they can convince a tribunal that they have acted within the legal interpretation of the contract, they will win the case. If a dispute starts to develop, ensure you follow the stipulations of the contract and that you keep written records of everything that happens, as well as sending notes and letters to the other party to confirm any meetings, discussions or agreements.

A classic mistake made by some homeowners when they fall out with a builder is immediately to prevent them from coming on to the site. This is an understandable reaction, but usually the contract will not give you the power to do this without following a set procedure. If you don't follow this procedure you could ultimately be the one who ends up out of pocket due to breach of contract, however wrong you think that the builder was in the first place. Always read the provisions in the contract that cover disputes or disagreements and follow them to the letter, however unpleasant it may feel.

If the other side behaves in an unreasonable way, you may be left with no option but to take them to court, but there are alternatives that should be considered first.

One comparatively recent innovation is called adjudication. It is automatically in place for all commercial contracts, whether or not there are written terms referring to it. It only applies to private householders' contracts if a clear written clause has been added. Either party can invoke the adjudication process and, once this is done, it can only be stopped if both parties agree. Otherwise, each presents their case to an adjudicator who is appointed by the organization named in the contract (e.g. RIBA). The adjudicator makes a decision, usually stating whether money is due to one side or the other, which has to be complied with. It is binding unless and until the dispute goes to a court or arbitrator, who can disregard it and make a different decision if they choose. Many disputes are settled by adjudication, because both sides get a small taste of what they will be in for if they end up in court.

Some contracts state that a dispute must go to an arbitrator, rather than a court. An arbitrator is trained and qualified to make decisions on legal disputes and acts as a judge in many ways, but has specialist knowledge about the construction industry, as well as flexibility regarding the running of the arbitration process. It was invented in the hope that it would be cheaper and quicker than a full-blown court case, but this has changed over the years since it was first brought in.

If your claim is valued at less than £5,000 (in 2011) you could consider the small claims court. This is a user-friendly procedure (as much as court can be) and you do not have to have a solicitor to represent you. Over this amount you will have to go to the County Court or High Court and accept the high costs that result.

Alternative dispute resolution, also known as mediation, is an option that tries to avoid the combative nature of legal action. The agreement of both parties to participate is necessary. A trained professional talks to both sides, establishes the common ground and tries to develop a compromise acceptable to both. Some of the professional bodies, such as the Royal Institute of British Architects (RIBA), offer this service, as well as independent bodies, such as the Centre for Effective Dispute Resolution (EDR). Judges are increasing keen on mediation, and litigants are directed to try it prior to moving on to a court case.

INSURANCE

There are several types of insurance cover needed by yourself and your team.

Professional Indemnity Insurance (PII)

This should be carried by your designer, engineer and other professional advisors. In the event of the professional being negligent, the insurer will pay any extra costs incurred by the client correcting the problem that results. In the legal sense, being 'wrong' is different from being 'negligent'. If the professional has had to make a judgement that turns out to be wrong, it is not negligent if a typical professional of the same type, in the same situation could have reasonably reached the same decision. This is because there are some aspects of a professional's work where an opinion must be formed, but it is not 100 per cent clear what to do. In these

cases there is a duty on the consultant at least to explain the risks to you.

If you come across someone who does not have indemnity insurance, do not employ them. Should they make an error or mistake, you will still have a legal right of redress but the usual defence is called 'man of straw' in legal circles, in other words they do not have enough assets to cover your costs should you be successful in a legal action against them, so it is not worth your while to pursue them.

It is perfectly reasonable to ask your professional to provide evidence that PII is in place and also that it is at the right level. If the cover is up to £50,000 for a project worth £45,000 this is still inadequate, since the consequences of negligence could affect the rest of the house; for example, if it burned down. Sometimes the providers of your finance will ask for certificates approving the work on site and they will not accept them from a professional who does not have PII in place. In these cases you should check they have adequate cover before you employ the designer to start work on the project.

Employer's Liability

All employers (builders, architects, subcontractors) must have insurance to cover their liability to their employees. This is to cover the costs that may result should an employee suffer injury or ill health. It is illegal not to have this cover if you employ anyone on a wage or salary. If you have any doubts about the honesty of the company you are dealing with, ask to see a certificate showing this cover is current and in place – this should be on display in their office.

Public Liability

This insurance covers any members of 'the public' who might get injured or whose property might get damaged as result of the building work. For example, if a friend visits your house whilst work is in progress and the builders damage the car, it covers the repair cost. If they are in the car and suffer an injury, it covers the compensation payments that may be due.

This insurance must be in place before the builders start work and you should ask to see a copy of their certificate. It usually provides cover for large sums, for example £5 million or £10 million, because the very worst cases can be very expensive.

If you decide to project manage the construction yourself, and there will be no builder taking responsibility for the management of the site, you should get this insurance to cover yourself.

House Insurance

This should already be in place, but it is very important to inform your insurance company when building work is about to start. This is because this type of policy has a clause that requires you to keep them informed of this situation. Whilst builders are working on the site there are increased risks for the insurer. Because strangers are coming and going around the house, it is easier for a burglar to enter the property without arousing the suspicions of neighbours. When parts of the existing fabric have been removed, the house may be insecure,

with access routes into it that cannot be locked. There is also an increased risk of damage to the existing house, or even fire. Provided that you tell the insurers, they will probably not increase your premium. If you forget to tell them and the worst happens, their terms and conditions allow them to refuse to cover the costs due to your non-disclosure of relevant facts.

THE PARTY WALL ACT

This legislation originated in London, where there are many complicated relationships between neighbouring buildings crammed together in small, densely populated areas. The party wall surveyors who administered it felt that it was so useful that they persuaded the government of the day to extend it to England and Wales. It is intended to resolve all disputes over building work in relation to party walls, boundary walls and excavations near neighbouring buildings. If your extension falls

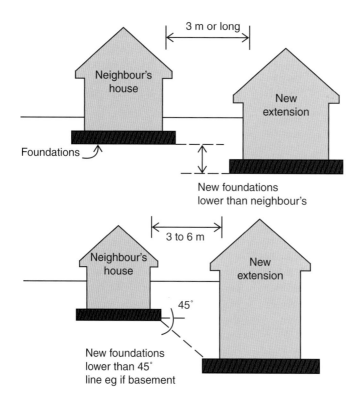

Two cases where the Party Wall Act applies.
Author.

in to any of the following categories, it will probably apply, and you will need your neighbour's written consent to proceed:

- If your new extension is within 3m of your neighbour's foundations and your foundations are likely to be lower than theirs.
- If your new foundations are between 3m and 6m from your neighbour's foundations and yours are deeper than a 45-degree line taken from the bottom of theirs.
- If a party wall (i.e. a wall that you both own half of) is affected by structural work, you will need their formal consent to alter it.
- If you intend to build along a boundary and your foundations will project under a neighbour's land, you have to serve a notice, but written consent is not required in this case.

The Act requires you to serve a formal written notice on an affected neighbour a month before work begins, giving details of what you intend to do. You cannot proceed until they have written back agreeing to the work. If the neighbour wishes to obstruct the project, they can object. Alternatively, if they do not respond for two weeks, they are assumed to dispute the proposals. If this happens, you have to appoint a surveyor to represent your interests and another one to represent the neighbour – but you foot the bill for both. If the two surveyors can't agree, yet another surveyor has to be appointed and paid by you to arbitrate. It is theoretically possible to get to this point without the neighbour doing or saying anything at all and also not having to pay anything towards the resultant costs.

So, if you wish to avoid lengthy and costly delays, it is best to meet your neighbours, show them your plans and address their concerns at an early stage. If the work is unlikely to cause a problem and your neighbour is amenable, it is possible to get them to sign the form without involving surveyors at all. Even if your neighbour decides to be awkward, once the party wall procedure has been followed, they must allow access for workmen and professional advisers to carry out the necessary work. As a last resort this right can be enforced though the courts. If you fail to follow the rules and start without getting consent from, or a settlement with, your neighbour, they can take out an injunction halting the work until the Party Wall Act provisions have been satisfied.

CHAPTER 11

Some Typical Extension and Alteration Projects

CASE STUDY: A CONTEMPORARY STYLE ADDITION TO A TRADITIONAL SUBURBAN HOUSE

House extension. Existing house from the rear.

Architect instructed: August 2010
Planning application submitted: September 2010
Tenders issued: November 2010
Start on site: January 2011
Completion: April 2011
Lowest tender: £38,000 plus VAT
Highest tender: £58,000 plus VAT
Architects: Julian Owen Associates
Project Architect: Nick Jones
Builder: A.S. Fearn Builders

This extension has been added to a typical suburban house in Nottingham. The brief was to increase the living space on the ground floor, to create a kitchen/dining/family room that is more in keeping with modern family life. The clients also wanted the new addition to reflect their taste for more contemporary style, without clashing with the appearance of the existing house. The design solution is simple and elegant, using traditional materials in a modern way. The design allows the new interior to be flooded with natural daylight and sunlight.

House extension. Existing house from the front.

House extension. New extension seen from the rear.

House extension. The new extension is very discrete from the front.

TOP: **House extension. The interior of the new extension.**

BELOW: **House extension. Elevations showing the house before and after.**

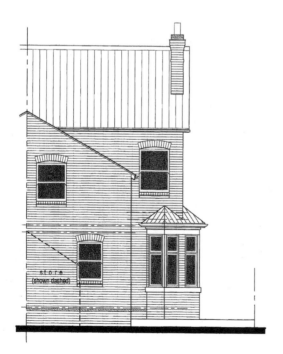

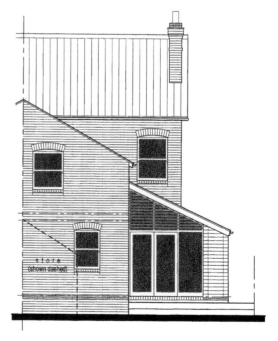

store
(shown dashed)

store
(shown dashed)

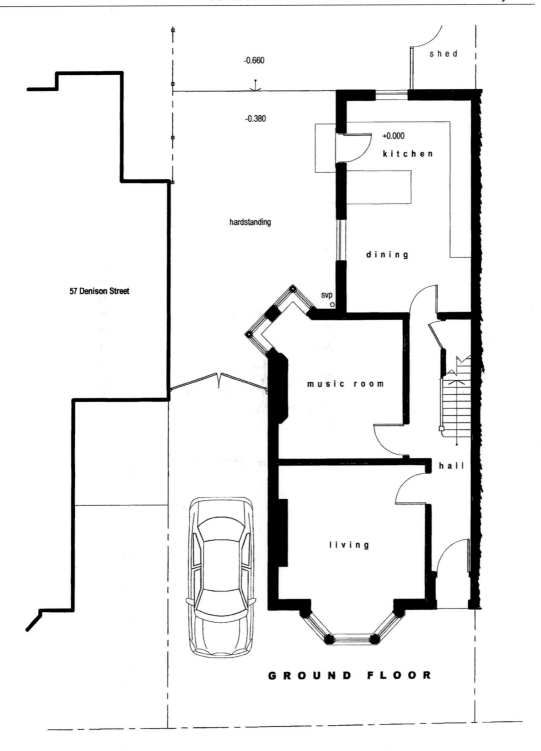

-0.660

-0.380

+0.000

s h e d

k i t c h e n

hardstanding

d i n i n g

57 Denison Street

svp

m u s i c r o o m

h a l l

l i v i n g

G R O U N D F L O O R

House extension. Ground-floor plan before the work was carried out.

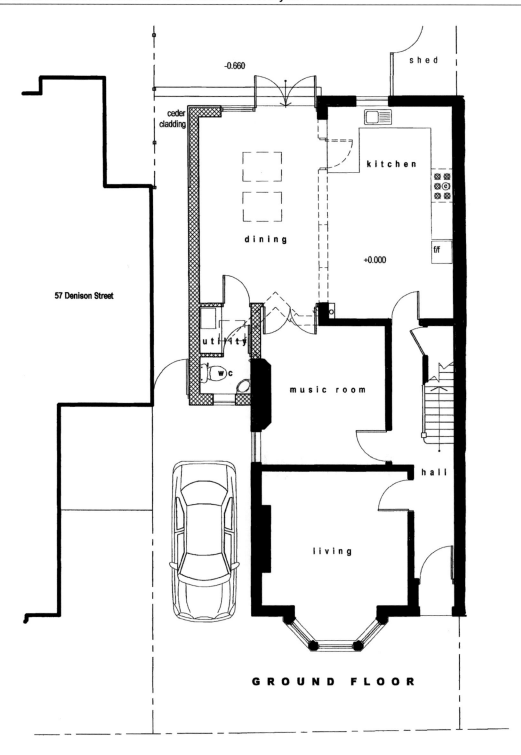

House extension. Ground-floor plan showing the proposed extension.

SOME OTHER EXAMPLES

The following are some examples of alterations to private homes.

House remodelling. Before.

House remodelling. After.

House extension 1 before the work was carried out.

House extension 1 after the work was completed.

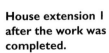

TOP: **House extension 2. Front of house before extending.**

BELOW: **House extension 2. Front of house after extending.**

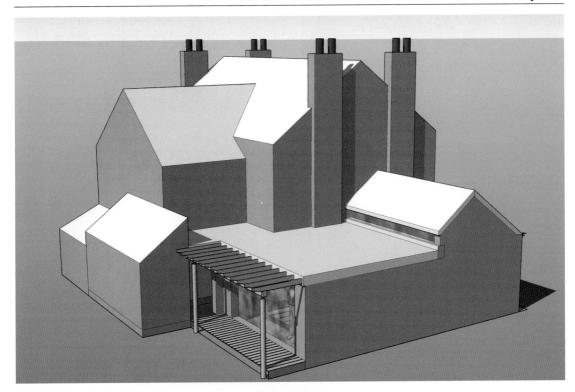

ABOVE: **House extension 2. Concept drawing of the proposed extension.**

RIGHT: **House extension 2. Rear of house after extending.**

House extension 2. Inside the new extension.

Recommended Reading

The Absolutely Essential Health and Safety Toolkit (Health and Safety Executive, 2002)
A useful site-friendly booklet with bullet points giving advice on the crucial health and safety issues on a typical small building site.

Build It Magazine (Inside Communications Media Ltd)
Lots of case studies and practical advice on building new and altering existing houses (www.buildit-online.co.uk).

Chilvers, P., Hill, D. and Owen, J. *Before You Build* (RIBA Publishing Ltd, 2007)
A short guide to the planning and building regulations, along with advice on how to approach the design and project management of a house alteration project.

Coulthard, S. *The 10 Best Ways to Add Value to Your House* (Pearson Education Ltd, 2008)
This book covers more than just loft conversions, but sets out how to assess whether your project is likely to make money in a direct and readable manner.

Coutts, J. *Loft Conversions* (Blackwell Publishing, 2006)
Designed more for professional builders and architects, this is a comprehensive guide to the practical side of loft conversions. A key source of the information in this book.

Dijksman, K. *The Planning Game* (Ovolo Publishing)
An excellent book on the planning system in the UK for householders, written in a frank style by a well-informed former local authority planning officer.

Elyahou, G *The Law for Home Improvers* (New Holland, 2004)
A through guide to all aspects of the law for home owners, including plenty of case studies.

Faulkner, K. *Developing Your Property* (Which? Ltd, 2007)
A concise, well-organized guide that give good advice on all aspects of alterations to individual houses.

Grand Designs Magazine (Media 10 Ltd)
A tie-in with the Channel Four TV series.

Grimaldi, P. *Getting the Builders In* (Elliot Right Way Books, 1993)
Useful tips on how to select, appoint and manage building contractors for alterations to your house.

Guidance on Unfair Term in Home Improvement Contracts (Office of Fair Trading)
Guide to some of the legislation that protects consumers. Available on the OFT website (www.oft.gov.uk)

Health and Safety in Construction (Health and Safety Executive, 2001)

A book that covers most of the health and safety issues on a building site with some advice on how they should be followed.

Homebulding and Renovating Magazine (Ascent Publishing Ltd)

A good quality publication that deals with all kinds of domestic building projects, including loft conversions (www.homebuilding.co.uk).

Hymers, P. *Home Conversions* (New Holland Publishers, UK Ltd, 2003)

A resonably priced paperback that covers all types of conversion, including lofts.

Liddell, H. *Eco-Minimalism* (RIBA Publishing, 2008)

A no-nonsense guide to the best and most effective options for building sustainably.

Mindham, C.N. *Roof Construction and Loft Conversion* (Wiley-Blackwell, 2006)

An excellent guide to the construction of loft conversions and the regulations that govern them. Aimed at construction professionals, but it would also be useful to anyone contemplating a DIY project. A key source of reference used in the preparation of this book.

Owen, J. *Home Extension Design* (RIBA Publishing Ltd, 2008)

A general guide to the design of house alterations, including advice on project management, by the author of this book.

Owen, J. *The Complete Loft Conversion Book* (Crowood, 2010)

By the author of this book. Offers detailed guidance on the design and construction of a loft conversion.

Pearson, D. *The Natural House Book* (Conran Octopus Ltd, 2000)

An excellent book for anyone interested in sustainable or 'green' building and designing for healthy living.

Phillips, R. *A Short Guide to Consumer Rights in Construction Contracts* (RIBA Publishing, 2010)

This is a very short introduction to the legislation that applies to construction projects for private houses.

The Property Makeover Price Guide (BCIS, 2007)

An excellent guide to approximate prices for getting items of building work completed to a home by a builder, with detailed price breakdowns as well as general costs per square metre for early estimating.

SelfBuild and Design Magazine (Waterways World Ltd)

A good source of ideas, in design terms as well as more practical matters (www.selfbuildanddesesign.co.uk).

Spain Spons, B. *House Improvement Price Book* (EandFN Spon)

A thorough breakdown of most of the likely costs for home improvement work. Used by the professionals and needs some understanding of the construction process.

Weiss, B. and Hellman, L. *Do It with an Architect* (Mitchell Beazley, 1999)

An excellent and humorous guide to getting the best out of your architect.

Useful Contacts

Acworth and Jarvis Architects
Mr Barny Acworth
6 Dean Park Crescent
Bournemouth
Dorset
BH1 1HL
01202 585540
www.acworthjarvis.co.uk

Architects Registration Board (ARB)
8 Weymouth Street
020 7580 5861
www.arb.org.uk
If you want to check whether a designer is a qualified architect, this is the organization to go to.

ASBA Architects
0800 387310
www.asba-architects.org
A national network of small architectural practices, whose members specialize in alterations and improvements to private houses.

A.S. Fearn Builders
Alan Fearn
1 Saxton Close
Beeston
Nottinghamshire
NG9 4DU

Association for Consultancy and Engineering
Alliance House
12 Caxton Street
London SW1H 0QL
020 7222 6557
www.acenet.co.uk
This organization will help you find a qualified structural engineer.

British Geological Society (BGS)
Records Section
0115 936 3143
enquiries@bgs.ac.uk
www.bgs.ac.uk
Details on subsoil and survey of the risk of radon gas. Lots of online maps of the geology of the UK.

British Woodworking Federation
020 7608 5050
www.bwf.org.uk
Run an accreditation scheme for installers of timber conservatories.

Chartered Institute of Architectural Technologists (CIAT)
020 7278 2206
www.ciat.org.uk
This body regulates architectural technicians and techonologists, who have to be qualified to be members.

Chartered Institute of Building
Englemere
Kings Ride
Ascot, Berkshire SL5 7TB
01344 630700
www.ciob.org.uk
This organisation is for contractors, who have to demonstrate knowledge, experience and qualifications to join.

Companies House
www.companieshouse.gov.uk
You can check a company's public accounts for a few pounds on this site.

Conservatory Association
44–48 Borough High Street
Southwark, London SE1 1XB
020 7207 5873
The Conservatory Association produces Minimum Technical Specifications and Recommended Code of Practice for conservatory construction and a list of member firms.

Energy Savings Trust
0800 512012
www.est.org.uk
A government-backed organization that was formed after the 1992 Rio Earth Summit. Its objectives are to achieve the sustainable use of energy in the UK and to reduce carbon emissions. The website has plenty of practical advice for home owners and businesses.

Experian
www.experian.co.uk
You can use this site to carry out credit checks on people, sole traders and companies.

FENSA Limited
FENSA Limited,
54 Ayres Street,
London, SE1 1EU
020 7645 3700
0870 780 2028
enquiries@fensa.org.uk
www.fensa.org.uk

FENSA stands for the Fenestration Self-Assessment Scheme. When having their windows and doors replaced, homeowners must ensure that they get a certificate form Local Authority Building Control or have the work completed by a FENSA Registered Company.

Health and Safety Executive
HSE Books
PO Box 1999
Sudbury
Suffolk CO10 2WA
01787 881165
www.hsebooks.com
Lots of free information on how to keep building sites safe.

Institution of Structural Engineers
The Institution of Structural Engineers
11 Upper Belgrave Street
London
SW1X 8BH
020 7235 4294
www.istructe.org

Joint Contracts Tribunal
www.jctltd.co.uk
This website has full details of various standard building contracts.

Julian Owen Associates Architects
Nottingham
0115 922 9831
www.julianowen.co.uk
The architectural practice run by the author, which has provided many of the photos for this book.

Nic Antony Architects
Mr Nic Anthony
Docklands Business Centre
10–16 Tiller Road
London
E14 8PX
020 7345 5070
www.nicantony.com

Royal Institute of British Architects (RIBA)
Client Services
66 Portland Place
London
W1B 1AD
020 7307 3700
www.ribafind.org
Will give enquirers a list of local architects who are RIBA members.

Royal Institution of Chartered Surveyors (RICS)
RICS Contact Centre
Surveyor Court
Westwood Way
Coventry
CV4 8JE
0870 333 1600
www.rics.org
This is the professional body for surveyors, who have to be qualified to gain membership.

The Land Registry (England and Wales)
020 7917 8888
www.landreg.gov.uk
You can use this site to find out who owns a given area of land or property and also look up the property prices for an area.

The Planning Inspectorate
Temple Quay House
2 The Square
Temple Quay
Bristol
BS1 6PN
0117 372 8000
www.planning-inspectorate.gov.uk
The Inspectorate deals with planning appeals.

The Planning Portal
www.planningportal.gov.uk
An organization set up by national government to act as an internet gateway for submitting planning applications. All online applications are made through this website, which records the submission details before forwarding them on to the relevant local authority. Also full of useful information on the planning rules and building regulations.

Glossary

Adjudication A quick and inexpensive method of dispute resolution resulting in an immediately enforceable, non-binding dispute settlement by an Adjudicator.

Approved Inspector The private, commercial equivalent of a local authority building control officer.

Architect, Registered Professional who has obtained sufficient qualifications to be registered with the government to use the title 'architect'.

Architectural Technologist Draughtsman who deals with the practical side of building design. Membership of the Chartered Institute of Architectural Technologists CIAT indicates training and qualifications.

Building Control Officer (BCO) Local authority official who checks buildings comply with the building regulations.

Building Regulations Minimum standards for construction and design, set by the government and illustrated by a series of booklets called Approved Documents.

Computer-Aided Design (CAD) Two- and three-dimensional models, created on computer, to give an idea of how a design may look and work out a schedule of components needed.

Dayworks Sheets These are formal records that should be kept of the man-hours spent by all the team on extra work and can be used as evidence of the amount that can be charged for labour.

Delegated Powers The process by which planning applications are decided without going to the local council's planning committee.

Damp-Proof Course (DPC) Prevents moisture rising up through the walls into a room.

Eaves The edge of a sloping roof, where the gutter is usually fixed.

Embodied Energy The energy that has been used to incorporate a material into a building, including the energy used manufacturing it, transporting it to the site and dealing with it after the building is demolished.

Estimate An informed guess, a rough price.

Fenestration Self-Assessment Scheme (FENSA) Allows contractors to install windows without requiring inspection by a Building Control Officer.

First Fix The point at which electric cables and pipework are put into position, usually once the building is watertight and before plastering.

Flashing Metal sheet used to deflect water at junction between roof and wall.

Gable Vertical triangular section of a wall, between two roof pitches.

Glazing Bar Horizontal support for a panel of glass in a window.

Hip Sloping section of roof between two other roof pitches. An alternative to a gable.

Jamb The side of an opening in a wall for a door or window.

JCT Contract Contract that has been produced by a collaboration of all the professionals involved in building work, including clients, builders and architects.

Joist Support for floor and ceiling.

Lintel Concrete, timber or steel beam over opening, to support wall above.

Low E Glass Glass that is treated to help to trap more heat from the sun in a room.

Making Good The finishing touches that bring work up to scratch, remedial work to existing surfaces and finishes affected by the work.

Ordnance Survey (OS) The only reliable source of larger scale maps, e.g. 1:1250.

Payback Period Period of time that a cost-saving measure needs to cover the initial cost, e.g. if extra insulation costs £500 to fit, and saves £100/year in fuel, the payback is five years.

Permitted Development Changes and additions that you can make to your house without needing formal planning approval from the local planning authority.

Pitch Slope of roof.

Procurement Route The way that a building project is managed, e.g. DIY, design and build.

Purlin Horizontal beam, part-way up a rafter, to prevent sagging.

Quote A fixed price that is binding.

Rafters Series of structural timbers rising from eaves to ridge to support pitched-roof covering.

RIBA Royal Institute of British Architects.

RICS Royal Institution of Chartered Surveyors.

Ridge Apex of a roof, where two pitches meet.

Roof Truss Prefabricated structural timber framework to support roof.

Second Fix The point at which radiators, sockets, switches, etc. are fixed, prior to decoration.

Solar Gain The build up of heat that occurs in a room when sun shines into it through glass.

Specification List of materials and procedures needed to complete a building, sometimes with a description of the standard of work that is expected.

Sustainable Construction Building in a way that reduces the damage that results to the environment. Similar to 'green' or 'environmentally friendly' building.

Trickle Ventilation Air that is allowed to flow into a room via adjustable grilles, usually fitted in window frames.

U-Value This number describes the insulative properties of a construction – the lower it is, the better it is at insulating.

Valley Line that follows the lowest point where two roof pitches meet.

Vernacular Design that uses the traditional building style and materials of a locality.

Index